Contents

Introduction

The trend away from the legal, clinical, and administrative segregation of the mentally ill was given official and public approval in the Mental Health Act 1959[1] which advocated that the emphasis in psychiatric care should be shifted as far as possible from the institution to care within the community. This principle ultimately led to the reassessment of the suitability and appropriateness of the traditional care given to the chronic psychiatric patient. The conclusions were voiced in the Hospital Plan for England and Wales[2] which established the rehabilitation and community care of the long-stay psychiatric patient as official policy. Since the Plan was issued the two questions which have continued to arouse considerable controversy are whether it is possible to restore the chronic patient socially, domestically and occupationally in the community, and if so at what cost to himself and the persons who become most responsible for his care.

Many have argued that the policy is dangerously superficial and does no more than represent the view of the anti-institution movement which fails to recognize the need for continuing hospital care for the majority of chronic patients. Further, they maintain that the majority of chronically disturbed patients are so emotionally handicapped and suffer such a degree of social poverty that they are not amenable to rehabilitation and should not, therefore, be cared for in the community but be allowed to spend their days in an institution. They believe that if care in the community is forced upon the chronic patient he will suffer from the dearth of local authority services, that relapse will quickly follow, and that during the exercise he will endure and cause undue hardship to those with whom he lives.

Contrary and more optimistic views stress the rehabilitation potential of chronic patients. They hold that chronic patients suffer very little from their original symptoms, present no particular problems, that their primary handicap is one of institutionalisation and dependency upon hospital routine, and that most should, and indeed could, be cared for in the community providing that alternative accommodation is available and given adequate support and facilities.

1

In truth the arguments for and against the community care of persons with chronic mental disorder are largely based upon opinion and the valuable studies and observation of the patient whilst he is still in the hospital. There have been few reports of the chronic patient and his actual behaviour, or of the problems he creates, if any, once he has left the institution. In consequence, the outcome of discharge and management in the community, for both the patient and the community, remains largely unknown and subject to conjecture.

The papers in this volume probe these questions by examining the evidence for and against looking after chronic psychiatric patients in non-hospital environments. In addition they relate the outcome of investigations and research into alternatives to hospital including care in day centres, hostels, group homes, boarding-houses and substitute family care. They also examine the role of local authorities and the voluntary sector in such schemes. They are presented in the belief that their findings demonstrate the validity of the aspirations contained in the 1962 Hospital Plan and in the conviction that "we need to revive the interest in meeting the needs of long-term patients in ways which are challenging and satisfying for both staff and patients, and which integrates such care with that of shorter stay patients.[3] (Para. 2.14).

M. ROLF OLSEN

References

1. *Mental Health Act 1959,* HMSO, London.
2. Ministry of Health, (1962), *The Hospital Plan for England and Wales,* HMSO, Cmnd; 1604, London.
3. *Better Services for the Mentally Ill,* (1975), D.H.S.S., HMSO, Cmnd; 6233, London.

1: A Review of the Evidence for and against the Discharge and Community Care of the Psychiatric Patient

M. Rolf Olsen

The Mental Hospital Population – A Prediction

In 1961 Tooth and Brooke,[1] in a now famous but controversial paper, predicted that by 1975 we would only require 1.8 psychiatric beds per thousand population compared with the 1954 peak, which represented about 3.4 beds per thousand population. They reported that in 1954 "many large schemes for new mental hospitals were under consideration", but by the end of 1955 there were indications that the steady increase in the size of the resident population had been reversed and that a corrected figure showed a drop of about 500. In spite of increasing admission and discharge rates, this trend continued, and by 1959 there were 8,000 fewer residents than in 1955. Tooth and Brooke felt that this decrease was accounted for by three factors: increasing use of out-patient treatment reducing the need for admission; earlier and more effective treatment in hospital lessening the need for prolonged care; active rehabilitation of the accumulated long-stay patients.

They felt that increased skill in the psychiatric hospitals and a developing community service would emphasise this trend, and estimated that discharges and deaths would account for all the long-stay patients "in about sixteen years". However, they thought it possible that a reverse effect might be created by increasing longevity and an increase in the numbers of old people with unmodifiable cerebral deterioration; the slowing down of the rehabilitation from long-stay wards as the hard core of organically deteriorated patients was reached; a change in community attitudes towards community care of the mentally ill; a deterioration in an economy which enabled a patient to be self-supporting.

In planning for the future, Tooth and Brooke separated the psychiatric bed requirement into three groups and estimated the following need – 340 short-stay beds, 530 medium-stay beds, and 890 long-stay beds – 1,760 beds per million population instead of the 3,400 beds per million population at the time of the report.

The Hospital Plan for England and Wales

In 1962 The Hospital Plan for England and Wales was issued.[2] It was based upon the predictions of Tooth and Brooke, and had, and still has, far reaching implications for the psychiatric services in general and the long-stay patient in particular.

The Plan assumed that during the next fifteen years the long-stay patients in mental hospitals would either be discharged or die, and further, that they would not be replaced on anything like the same scale. It was envisaged that a greater number of patients would receive short-stay care in psychiatric units based upon the new general hospitals, and that a greater proportion of patients would receive care within the community. In consequence, it was felt that a number of hospitals would close and that the remainder would reduce in size. There were no plans to build further mental hospitals.

In effect the proposals of the Hospital Plan, reinforced by new drugs, new skills, changing attitudes and the developing social services, established the rehabilitation and community care of long-stay patients as official policy.

The Controversy

Both the Plan and the Paper upon which it was based aroused opposing views supported by conflicting evidence.

Its supporters, although differing in their estimates for the size of run down and length of time it would take, generally saw it as an imaginative bold policy that would do much to remedy the handicaps common to most hospitals. In particular, their custodial image, geographical isolation, and out-dated unsuitable premises. In the long run it was felt it would boost flagging staff morale and that a better recruit would be attracted; the new units, centred upon general hospitals, would be more acceptable to the patient and would act as a focus for community-based psychiatry.

Norton (1961)[3], in his survey of female patients admitted to a mental hospital during the past thirty years found that, whilst the number admitted had risen fourfold, the median length of stay for schizophrenics who were discharged had fallen from seven months to nine weeks, and for endogenous depression and manic depressive psychosis from six months to seven weeks. On the other hand, patients with senile and arteriosclerotic dementia accounted for one-twelfth of all admissions and only 10 per cent were discharged. Dementia had replaced schizophrenia as the commonest cause of long-term hospital care. Norton felt that the decrease in the number of schizophrenic illnesses becoming chronic might lead to a fall in the total patient population of 30 per cent by 1981. If, in addition, changes in national policy were effective, then he felt mental hospitals may be reduced to one-quarter of their size.

Cooper and Early (1961)[4], surveyed all the patients who had been in longer than three months at the Glenside Hospital, Bristol, with particular reference to their need for accommodation and employment outside hospital. They found that of 1,012 patients, 453 men and 559 women, surveyed, 85.2 per cent had been in hospital continuously for two years or more. In assessing the need for supervision the authors felt that 122 patients did not require supervision of any kind and that a further 355 required only the minimal supervision normally provided in a long-stay annexe or after-care hostel.

In relation to the patient's employment needs, Cooper and Early found that 279 patients (29.3%) were being paid by outside employers and that only 372 (36.7%) were totally unemployed.

Cross and Yates (1961)[5], in their census of patients in residence in four Birmingham hospitals, gave much the same prediction as Tooth and Brooke of 340 short-stay beds and 600 continued treatment beds per million population, but estimated a need for 11 per cent more long-stay beds.

Early and Magnus (1966)[6], carried out a mental hospital survey to determine the changes which had taken place during the previous four years, and to ascertain the rate of rundown of hospital beds. Their survey revealed an overall decline of 6.4 per cent, and long-stay patients showed a more rapid decline by death and discharge than predicted by Tooth and Brooke.

Magnus (1967)[7], found that in the six years since the 1961 Cooper and Early review at Glenside Hospital, a considerable number of new admissions had been continuously in hospital for over a year. To assess the size and characteristics of this group, Magnus applied a questionnaire to all new patients admitted between 1961 and 1966 who had been resident for more than one year and were still resident in hospital at the time of the review. He found that of the 178 reviewed, 112 (62%) had been in hospital for more than two years. Interviews with patients and nursing staff, and review of the family and domestic situations, led Magnus to conclude that:—

"Only half these patients required to remain in hospital for psychiatric reasons. The remainder could be accommodated in hostels for the after-care, or in hostels for the elderly infirm, if such facilities existed."

Magnus went on to say that the area Local Authority hostel was only being used to half capacity and unless greater understanding existed between Local

Authority and Hospital, and utilisation of the patient's own family, as described by Rawnsley, London and Miles (1962)[8], took place, then:—

"it is doubtful whether the anticipated 1.8 beds/1,000 population as laid down by the Ministry of Health (1962) will be sufficient for future needs."

Rawnsley et al (1962) assessed the attitudes of relatives to a family member in a mental hospital and found that 28 per cent of the sample of 230 patients had not been visited for over a year, and 20 per cent had been without any form of contact with their families. In spite of this they estimated that 60 per cent of the study group and 24 per cent of those patients without a visitor for a year or more were found to have relatives willing to offer accommodation on discharge.

Falling hospital populations have caused similar excitement in America. Brill and Paton (1957)[9], reported that on 31st March 1954, there were 90,839 patients in the New York State Mental Hospitals, over double the number of twenty-five years before, and four times the 1900 figure. During the year there had been an increase of 2,500 patients, and the average rise during the previous decade was 2,000 per annum. However, during the year 1955-56 there was a fall of some 500 patients which the authors attributed to the large scale use of Chlorpromozine.

In 1959[10], the same authors repeated the study and showed that the fall had continued. On 31st March the population was 4,100 below the figure of 1955, when it could have been expected to hav been 8,000 – 10,000 higher. However, on completion of the second study Brill and Paton felt that the population fall was not solely attributable to drug therapy but to a whole series of changes in practice and staff attitudes that had taken place.

Criticism was levelled at the Plan on many fronts. It was questioned whether it was legitimate to plan on what had happened during the previous five years of extraordinary development, and whether adequate allowance had been made for the expected increase in psycho-geriatric cases. It was claimed that insufficient consideration had been given to regional variations, a criticism born out by the Statistical Report, Series No. 12, (1969)[11]. Some have stressed the limitations of drugs and others were doubtful about the practicability of rehabilitating large numbers of long-stay patients, many of whom were schizophrenic. Emphasis had been laid on the limited capacities of long-stay patients and the anticipated social problems and family upheaval that they would create. It was felt erroneous to assume the number occupying beds indicated need.

Some opinion and research indicate that the consequence of this policy are to the detriment of the patient and his community, and challenge whether it is cheaper than hospital care or more humane to reject the patient from the institution that has become his home.

Gore and Jones (1961)[12], did not share Cooper and Early's optimism for the employment and discharge of long-stay patients and carried out a patient census at the large mental hospital, Menston, Yorkshire, "a hospital compelled to adopt in the main a custodial form of care", to examine the nature of the long-stay patient and his potential for rehabilitation; 68.6 per cent of the 1,133 men and 62.7 per cent of the 1,218 women had been in hospital in excess of five years. Of this long-stay group, 77.22 per cent of the men and 57.98 per cent of the women were under 65 years of age, and "many still in their 30's and 40's". The authors calculated:—

"on the basis of the General Register Office abridged life table for 1957-1959, and assuming that the average life span of a long-stay patient does not differ from that of the general community, it is calculated that a minimum of 651 of these 1,541 would still be alive in sixteen years time."

In calculating the size of the chronic population in sixteen years, this estimate took no consideration of how fast the chronic population was replacing itself.

Gore and Jones thought that discharge to the community was not a viable proposition for the majority of patients. They found that half the long-stay patients, 48.91 per cent of the men and 48.17 per cent of the women, were only working on their own wards, and that a further large proportion, 27.41 per cent male and 36.65 per cent female, were not carrying out even minor tasks. They felt that the "overwhelming majority would not be capable of sustaining paid employment in the community". Less than 20 per cent of the men and women had a marriage partner to return to if they were discharged, and 32.75 per cent of the men and 30.51 per cent of the women never had a visitor of any kind. This evidence suggests, that in this hospital at least, the assumption "that none of the long-stay patients will remain in sixteen years" is unlikely to be fulfilled.

Jones and Sidebotham (1962)[13], did not accept that the falling population curve would continue "of its momentum until the mental hospitals are empty"; neither did they accept that, just because present mental hospitals were considered to be unsatisfactory, it would mean that money would be available to hasten the development of community services or psychiatric beds in general hospitals. They felt that the consequence of the Hospital Plan would be for able staff to leave the mental hospitals; research and clinical advance would be slowed by lack of facilities and the staff exodus; and that as mental hospitals decline in their status they would become the dumping ground for the less attractive case.

Hill (1962)[14], raised the question of whether:—

"with the use of more powerful tranquillizers and with the use of more efficient social services we shall become increasingly blinded to our really profound ignorance about what we are doing."

He felt that:—

"a new empiricism seems to have evolved in psychiatry in which the aim is to cure the symptoms rather than the development of understanding of the illnesses which give rise to them, which should lead ultimately to the control and prevention of these illnesses."

Mandlebrote (1964)[15], speaking about care within the community felt:—

"there is still a great deal of anxiety about the consequences it may have for the community. One of the major anxieties has been the effect that it may have in increasing the burden on the family and community, where chronic illness has been inadequately alleviated."

Rehin and Martin (1963)[16], made their challenge to the Plan on four major issues which they felt underlined the proposals:—

(1) that the necessary limit of beds may be estimated statistically,

(2) that regional variations need not be taken into account,

(3) that a new balance should be established between mental and general hospitals,

(4) that the contribution of the community and its tolerance is not relevant to criticism.

This P.E.P. study gave a sound basis for its criticisms and concluded that "the statisticians have measured usage which has innumerable determinants, the planners appear to have assumed with no evident justification that this may be taken as a measure of need". They thought that the statistical basis for the Ministry's predictions had placed "unrealistic reliance upon an extraordinary period in the evolution of psychiatric services" and that this "aspect of the Hospital Plan is particularly open to criticism".

They found that in 1960, psychiatric provision in different regions ranged from 2.3 to 7.2 beds per 1,000 population. The Plan did not allow for the regional variations. Rehin and Martin concluded that:—

"it would be unfortunate if arbitrary application of a not very sophisticated formula were to impose a pattern of usage which in many areas would be quite unrelated to medical or social need."

Further, they pointed out, these figures took no account of extra or new demand that might be created.

When considering the development of psychiatric units in general hospitals they shared the view of Jones and Sidebotham (1962)[13], and thought the new units would cream off the therapeutic potential to the disadvantage of the traditional hospital.

In the absence of any published ten-year plan by the Local Authorities to match the Hospital Plan, the authors felt:—

"it is a matter of great regret that their future has not been considered within the same framework as the development of the hospital psychiatric services."

The study warned of the lack of knowledge about the inter-relationship between hospitals and community services and the possibility of an unacceptable burden being placed on the Local Authority services by the rundown of the hospitals.

Norton (1961)[17], and Lindsay (1962)[18], also criticised Tooth and Brooke's statistical interpretation, and both felt that depopulation of the hospitals would take far longer than envisaged, and that future needs for psychiatric beds cannot be estimated by applying a national trend to a local area.

Spencer, Cross and Hassall (1965)[19], state that a yardstick of this sort may be grossly misleading because it presumes that existing populations in different hospitals will change in the same way. To test this hypothesis they recorded all patients in one hospital at the end of the years 1952, 1957 and 1960. The patients were then followed up at the end of 1962. Comparing the results with those available from other hospitals it was clear that the way in which numbers fall depends upon the age structure and length of stay of the patients in each hospital. Both these factors vary from one hospital to another. They claim that, to make a realistic forecast, surveys should be carried out in all psychiatric hospitals and that the findings provide the basis for regional planning.

In his report for 1968, The Chief Medical Officer of the Department of Health and Social Security[20], confirmed the findings of Spencer, Cross and

Hassall, and reported that, although bed numbers in some areas were already below the predicted 1.8 per 1,000 population, the rundown had not occurred in others. He concluded that when bed numbers fail to fall a number of factors were at work, in particular, a number of hospitals were taking an increased load of geriatric patients and relieving deficiencies in Local Authority provisions for the elderly.

The Stastitical Report on Psychiatric Hospitals and Units in England and Wales, Series No. 12, (1969)[11], found that, whilst the numbers of in-patients had fallen nationally and in each region, the reduction has not been uniform between one region and another – indeed the disparities in 1969 were in some respects greater than those which existed in 1954. The three regions with most in-patients per 1,000 population were Leeds 2.64, South-Western 2.72, and Liverpool 3.03. The three with least in-patients were Oxford, 1.57 Sheffield 1.75, and Manchester 1.91. For Wales as a whole the ratio was 2.39.

The Report estimated that, whilst the number of in-patients for every 1,000 population had fallen by 31 per cent between 1954 and 1969, if the current pattern of psychiatric care continued an extra 8,000 or 9,000 beds would be required, mostly for people aged 75 and over, during the next decade.

Hassall and Hellon (1964)[21], in view of the divergent conclusions drawn by Gore and Jones, and Cooper and Early, carried out a further survey of a long-stay hospital population at an adequately staffed non-custodial psychiatric hospital, in the hope of clarifying the position, particularly in relation to the accommodation needs of the long-stay group. Of the 576 patients, 70.5 per cent were long-stay; 60.5 per cent were aged less than 65 years; even though work was available, 23.6 per cent of the males and 37.6 per cent of the females were unemployed; 79.6 per cent of the men and 83.5 per cent of the women were without spouses; 27.2 per cent of the males and 39.2 per cent of the females did not leave hospital and had no contact with relatives.

This study, like Gore and Jones, conveyed the sense of social isolation and the degree of handicap confronting many of these patients which mitigates against successful rehabilitation, whilst at the same time the life expectancy of many was great.

Catterson, Bennett and Freudenberg (1963)[22], in a survey of the functional handicaps of a sample of 75 male and 75 female long-stay schizophrenic patients under 60 years of age, rated four symptoms – flatness of affect, poverty of speech, incoherence of speech and coherently expressed delusions – on a five-point scale of severity. Forty-five per cent were judged to be moderately ill clinically, only 13 per cent could be considered for discharge, and that the remainder "were too disabled to justify asking their relatives to look after them". The authors were doubtful about the practicability of rehabilitating large numbers of chronic patients.

May, Gregory, Jones and Bruggen (1963)[23], considered that:—

"the desire to help patients who have been in hospital for over two years is laudable, but an aggressive policy of discharge at any price can bring disaster and disappointment to patient and family alike",

and that to force the patient back into the community would invite rejection. They advocated the need for long-stay patients to pass through a rehabilitation unit prior to discharge which would offer continued support following departure from hospital.

The Long-stay Patient: His Rehabilitation Potential

This brief review of the evidence shows that the controversy aroused by the 1962 Hospital Plan originated in contradictory descriptions of the long-stay patient, in the opposing conclusions about his social and clinical needs, and in the disagreement over his potential for rehabilitation.

A number of researchers claim that the majority of long-stay patients require very little care or supervision and state that many could, and indeed should, return to the community. Other findings stress the limited capacities of this group and assert that sustained living in an undemanding institutional environment has produced an individual who is not amenable to rehabilitation, and conclude therefore, that he should be allowed to live out his days in the institution that has become his home.

The Long-stay Patient: His Meagre Rehabilitation Potential

The second view, which stresses the social handicap of the long-stay patient, was supported by Myerson (1939)[24], who felt that chronic schizophrenics, who make up about two-thirds of the long-stay patient group in a psychiatric hospital, are in a state similar to 'prison stupor'. In this condition the patient withdraws from social contact into delusions, with catatonic stupor representing the extreme form of retreat. Myerson described the particular features of this condition as withdrawal, solitariness, lowered initiative and passivity symptoms which are emphasised by the 'motivation and psychological vacuum' devoid of reward, punishment and stimulation which is characteristic of the long-stay ward in which he lives.

Barton (1959)[25], gives a similar description in his exposition on institutionalisation, in which he coined the phrase 'institutional neurosis' to describe the personality changes that take place. He states that the chronic patient is characterised by apathy, lack of initiative, loss of interest, submissiveness, a loss of individuality, and a resigned acceptance of everything around him. The patient often adopts a typical posture with limited physical movement. Barton was uncertain as to the cause of this inertia but felt that factors 'commonly found' contributing to it are:— loss of contact with the outside world; enforced idleness; 'bossiness' by the medical and nursing staff; loss of personal friends, possessions and personal events; drugs; negative ward atmosphere and loss of prospects.

Goffman (1961)[26], felt that the aetiology of 'institutional neurosis' is to be found in the very nature of the 'total institution'.

"In short, mental hospitalization out-manoeuvres the patient, tending to rob him of the common expressions through which people hold off the embrace of organizations – insolence, silence, sotto voce remarks, unco-operativeness, malicious destruction of interior decorations, and so forth; these signs of disaffiliation are now read as signs of their maker's proper affiliation."

Other studies supporting the descriptions by Myerson and Barton and which conclude a meagre rehabilitation potential of chronic patients have already been mentioned. In particular:—

Gore and Jones (1961)[12], who considered that discharge to the community was not a viable proposition for the majority of long-stay patients.

Hassall and Hellon (1964)[21], like Gore and Jones, conveyed the same sense of social isolation and handicap confronting many of the long-stay patients which mitigates against successful rehabilitation.

Catterson, Bennett and Freundenberg (1963)[22], in their survey of the functional handicaps in a sample of long-stay patients, felt that only 13 per cent could be considered for discharge and that the remainder 'were too disabled to justify asking their relatives to look after them'.

In addition, Waters and Northover (1965)[27], in their assessment of a hospital pre-discharge rehabilitation programme, designed for long-stay schizophrenics, concluded that the value of the unit 'seemed almost entirely in terms of minimizing their secondary handicaps'.

A similar picture is given in an American study, carried out by Morgan and Johnson (1957)[28], which described the characteristics of 1,031 male and 1,135 female patients who had resided in the Warren State Hospital for two years or more. They found that schizophrenia accounted for two-thirds of the chronic group. The median age for males was 53 years and for females 57 years; the median hospital stay for the men was 11 years and for the women 14 years; 28 patients had been in hospital continuously for more than 44 years – the oldest had been in 61 years. On these findings it was anticipated that some of the patients admitted in 1956 would still be in hospital in the year 2,000. Most of the chronic patients had a poor educational and employment background – only 0.8 per cent of the chronic group had a professional background. At the time of admission there was an absence of 'first line relatives', only 22 per cent of the male and 34 per cent of the females were married – a proportion that was smaller at the time of investigation since some of the patients will have been separated, divorced or widowed during admission. Only 23 per cent of the males and 27 per cent of the females had both parents living. Although 91 per cent of the group had at least one sibling (80 per cent had two or more) on admission, very little interest was shown by them. At the time of investigation 10 per cent were visited regularly but a third never received visits of any kind. Only 8 per cent of the patients had twenty dollars or more in their personal account, whilst 69 per cent had no personal spending money at all.

In summary, the chronic male patient in this study has a median age of 53 years, a median duration of stay of 11 years, is probably unmarried and without children, has a probability of one in five of having both parents alive, and has a poor educational and employment background. If he has relatives alive they show scant interest. He is poor. Almost the same profile could be drawn for the females.

This absence of 'first line' relatives and consequent social isolation has been noted by a number of workers such as Ødegard (1946)[29] and Norris (1956)[30], who have shown that hospital admission rates for the single person are greater than for married persons and that once in hospital the single stay longer than the married. This phenomenon is found in all age and diagnostic groups, but is particularly marked for the major psychoses, schizophrenia and manic depressive psychoses.

The Long-stay Patient: His Latent Potentiality for Discharge

Contrary and more optimistic findings, stressing the rehabilitation potential of many long-stay patients, have been stated by a number of authors. In general they claim that about half the long-stay patient population could be discharged with the minimum of difficulty providing alternative accommodation was available.

Cross, Harrington and Mayer-Gross (1957)[31], in their study of 442 male and 654 female long-stay psychiatric patients in a mental hospital, found that two-thirds of the males and three-quarters of the females had been resident for ten years or more. Half of the study group did not present any marked behaviour problem and the authors concluded that retention in hospital often depended upon social factors rather than clinical need. Using a fourfold classification to assess the nursing needs of this long-stay group, the authors concluded that 'only a very small proportion of patients required constant vigilance and about two-thirds required routine care only'. In this study it was felt that the degree of supervision given to patients depends not only on the mental state of the individual patient but on the ward tradition and administrative policy.

Garratt, Lowe and McKeown (1959)[32] assessed the medical and social needs of 3,555 psychiatric patients in four Birmingham mental hospitals and found that only 13 per cent of the patients required the full range of hospital facilities; 75 per cent required only limited hospital services; the remaining 12 per cent, 441 patients, required no hospital care whatsoever; 84 per cent of the total group were fully ambulent. The authors stressed the need to reorganize the accommodation for patients, based upon their psychiatric and social needs, and to provide accommodation that gives the minimum of supervision and support.

The findings of Cooper and Early (1961)[4] have already been discussed. It is sufficient to reiterate that they considered that out of 1,012 patients in Glenside Hospital, 85.2 per cent of whom were long-stay, 122 required no nursing care, and 355 only minimum nursing care – a total of 47.1 per cent who were not in need of hospitalization.

Magnus (1967)[7], in his review of 178 patients of whom 112 (62%) had been in hospital for two years or more and the remainder for more than one year, concluded that half could be discharged to hostels if such places were available.

Conclusion

The Hospital Plan, 1962, and the prediction upon which it was based, produced opposing conclusions. One view rejected the feasibility of community care, maintaining that long-stay patients are not amenable to the rehabilitation, that relapse will quickly follow discharge, and that during the exercise the patient will cause undue hardship to his living group. The opposite view holds that long-stay patients suffer very little from their original symptoms, that they present no particular problems, that their primary handicap is one of institutionalisation and dependency upon hospital routine, and that most could be discharged with adequate support and facilities.

These conflicting opinions in part arise as a result of a too narrow perspective and a failure to consider the total situation. The institutionalists, in focusing upon the destructive effect of institutionalisation on an individual, conclude a meagre rehabilitation potential. On the other hand the alleviators give insufficient consideration to the nullifying effect of the institution. Neither group has taken the whole of the evidence into consideration, and little is known about the effect of discharge upon the long-stay patient. In consequence, the outcome of discharge, for both the patient and the community, remains largely unknown and subject to conjecture.

In truth the arguments for and against the Plan are largely based upon opinion and studies on the patient whilst he is still in hospital. Little is known about the chronic patient and his actual behaviour, or the problems he creates, if any, once he has left the institution.

Events have shown that the crucial question is not whether the policies to discharge long-stay patients or to maintain psychiatric patients in the community is possible, for we know they are, but whether such strategies are desirable and in the best interests of the patient and the community. This evaluation is dependent upon a number of factors including investigation of the post-discharge experiences and outcome. At the moment our understanding of the rehabilitation process is meagre and our knowledge of the factors which affect it is conflicting. We are aware that there are powerful social factors which influence its outcome, but so far only the broad lines are to be seen and our ignorance of its complexities is great. However, the magnitude of the problems presented by the large numbers of psychiatric long-stay patients occupying hospital beds – often for the greater part of their lives – makes it imperative that we assess whether it is possible to restore and maintain the patient in the community. From several points of view the gains to be made by successful rehabilitation appear to be considerable, not least the financial saving, the economic use of scarce resources, a more humane care for the patient with opportunity to re-establish his identity as a person, and last but not least, an improvement in the morale of hospital and community-based staff who have the opportunity to see themselves in a therapeutic rather than custodial role.

It is hoped that the papers in this volume, which report the findings of research into alternative systems to hospital care, will contribute to that analysis.

References

1. Tooth, G. C. and Brooke, E. M. (1961) Trends in the Mental Hospital Population, *Lancet,* 1.4.61, 710-713.
2. Ministry of Health (1962), The Hospital Plan for England and Wales, HMSO, Cmnd. 1604.
3. Norton, A. (1961), Mental Hospital Ins and Outs, *Brit.Med. J.,* 25.2.61, 528-36.
4. Cooper, K. W. and Early, D. F. (1960), Review of a Hospital Population, *Brit.Med.J.,* 1600-1603.
5. Cross, K. W. and Yates, J. (1961), Follow-up Study of Admissions to Mental Hospitals, *Lancet,* 6.5.61, 1989-91.
6. Early, D. F. and Magnus, R. V. (1966), Population Trends in a Mental Hospital, *Brit.J. Psychiat.,* 112, 595-601.
7. Magnus, R. V. (1967), The New Chronics, *Brit.J.Psychiat.,* 113, 555-6.
8. Rawnsley, K. Loudon, J. B. and Hiles, H. L. (1962), Attitudes of Relatives to Patients in Mental Hospital, *Brit.J.Prev.Soc.Med.,* 16, 1.
9. Brill, K., and Paton, R. E. (1957), Analysis of 1955-56 Population Fall in New York State Mental Hospital in First Year of Large-scale Use of Tranquilising Drugs, *Am.J.Psychiat.,* 114, 6, 509.
10. Brill, K. and Paton, R. E. (1959), Analysis of Population Reduction in New York State Mental Hospital during First Four Years of Large-scale Therapy with Psychotropic Drugs, *Am.J.Psychiat.,* 116, 6, 465.
11. Psychiatric Hospitals and Units in England and Wales. Important Statistics from the Health Inquiry for 1969. Statistical Report, Series No. 12, HMSO.
12. Gore, C. & Jones, K. (1961), Survey of a Long-stay Mental Hospital Population, *Lancet,* 544-46.
13. Jones, K. and Sidebotham, R. (1962), *Mental Hospitals at Work,* Routledge & Kegan Paul.
14. Hill, D. (1962), The Burden on the Community: The Epidemiology of Mental Illness. A Symposium, published for Nuffield Provincial Hospitals Trust by OUP.
15. Mandelbrote, B. M. (1964), 'Mental Illness in Hospital and Community: Developments and Outcome', in *Problems and Progress in Medical Care,* published for Nuffield Provincial Hospital Trust by OUP.
16. Rehin, G. F. and Martin, F. M. (1963), *Psychiatric Services in 1975,* PEP, London.
17. Norton, A. (1961), 'Needs and Beds', Letter to *Lancet,* 22.4.61, 1, 884.
18. Lindsay, J. S. B. (1962), 'Trends in Mental Hospital Populations and the Effect on Planning', Letter to *Lancet,* 23.6.62, 1, 1354-5.
19. Spencer, A. M., Hassall, C. and Cross, K. W. (1965), Some Changes in the Composition of a Mental Hospital Population, *Brit.J.Psychiat.* 111, 420-428.
20. Annual Report of the Chief Medical Officer, Department of Health & Social Security (1968).
21. Hassall, C. and Hellon, C. P. (1964), Survey of a Long-stay Population at a Psychiatric Hospital, *Brit.J.Psychiat.,* 110, 183-85.

22. Catterson, A. G., Bennett, D. H. and Freudenberg, R. K. (1963), A Survey of Long-stay Schizophrenic Patients, *Brit.J.Psychiat.,* 109, 750.

23. May, A. R., Gregory, D. M. H., Jones, P. M. and Bruggen, P. (1963), Returning the Psychiatrically Disabled to the Community, *Lancet,* ii, 3.8.63, 241-43.

24. Myerson, A. (1939), Theory and Principles of the 'Total Push' Method in the Treatment of Chronic Schizophrenia, *Am.J.Psychiat.,* 95, 1198-1204.

25. Barton, R. (1959), *Institutional Neurosis,* J. Wright & Sons Ltd., Bristol.

26. Goffman, E. (1961), *Asylums: Essays on the Social Situation of Mental Patients and Other Inmates,* Pelican.

27. Waters, M. A. and Northover, J. (1965), Rehabilitated Schizophrenics in the Community, *Brit.J.Psychiat.* iii, 258-267.

28. Morgan, N. C. and Johnson, N. A. (1957) Failures in Psychiatry, *Am.J.Psychiat.,* 113, 9, 824-830.

29. ødegard, O. (1946), Marriage and Mental Disease, *J.Ment.Sci.,* 92, 35-39.

30. Norris, V. (1956), A Statistical Study of the Influence of Marriage on the Hospital Care of the Mentally Sick, *J.Ment.Sci.,* 102, 428, 467-486.

31. Cross, K. W., Harrington, J. A. and Meyer-Gross, W. (1957), A Survey of Chronic Patients in a Mental Hospital, *J.Ment.Sci.,* 103, 430, 146-169.

32. Garrett, F. N., Lowe, C. R. and McKeown, T. (1959), Institutional Care of the Mentally Ill, *Lancet,* i, 29.3.59, 682-683.

PART TWO

TECHNIQUES TO IMPROVE SOCIAL FUNCTIONING

2: The Chronic Psychiatric Patient – Techniques to Improve Social Functioning
M. Rolf Olsen

Introduction

In the previous chapter I related the conflicting findings in the descriptions of long-stay patients, and the opposing views regarding the possibility or rightness of discharging appreciable numbers to the community.

An important consideration in this issue is whether it is possible to improve the social functioning of persons with chronic psychiatric disabilities. Throughout the 1950s there were a number of key papers which reported the results of experiments to enhance social functioning of long-stay patients whilst still in the institution. These have importance for all schemes which aim to maintain psychiatric patients in the community, not only because they indicate whether successful rehabilitation might be possible but also because they suggest techniques which might lessen the effects of institutionalisation described by Barton (1959)[1] and others.

The experiments have tended to concentrate on three major areas of treatment and activity including:— work and occupational therapy; social therapy; and drug therapy.

Work and Occupational Therapy

In the late 1920s and during the early 1930s the value of occupational and work therapy, in the management of psychiatric patients, was beginning to be recognized. As it gained importance in psychiatry so its use in Europe was studied by a number of observers.

Evans (1929)[2], following a tour of eight Dutch hospitals and clinics, described a situation that was in advance of practice in the United Kingdom. At the Maasoord Hospital, accommodating 900 patients, he found that all patients not confined to bed were 'quietly occupied' on a variety of tasks. Continuous tasks took the place of the padded cell and, although the windows contained more glass than British psychiatric hospitals, 'window smashing is almost unknown'. At Sanport Hospital, then the largest of the Dutch Mental Hospitals, accommodating 1,500 patients, occupational and work therapy

23

was also extensively used. At the University Clinic, Amsterdam, containing 200 beds for neurological and mental patients without certification, 'social prophylaxes is kept to the fore'. In reviewing his overall impressions of the tour, Dr. Evans noted the 'quiet industry' and absence of noise or introspective idleness. Open wards which patients entered voluntarily made a deep impression.

During a further tour of nine hospitals and clinics in Western Germany, Evans (1933)[3] confirmed his earlier views established during his tour of Holland, that where employment of patients is thoroughly taken in hand 'the wards are quiet and free from excess motor activity and there is a great reduction of dirty and destructive habits'.

Unfortunately, this early British interest in occupational therapy was not to survive the impact made by the arrival of the physical methods of treatment. Indeed, at one time, work therapy was often interpreted as the exploitation of cheap labour. Many hospitals during this time gave up their farms, which – if they had been developed upon enlightened lines – might have provided ideal sheltered and training workshops.

Carstairs, Clark and O'Connor (1955)[4] thought that the revival of interest in occupational therapy during the early 1950s 'is perhaps the result of a more sober assessment of the limitations of physical treatment'. The authors made a tour of Holland, Belgium and France with the aim of studying current European practice in the rehabilitation of the chronic psychotics, by assessing:—

(a) the material and psychological setting,

(b) the types of work carried out,

(c) the principles on which the work therapy was organized.

In Holland they found that the leading practice was based on the work of Dr. Hermann Simon, a pioneer of active treatment in mental hospitals. His philosophy was based on the conviction that inactivity and frequent exposure to the spectacle of degraded behaviour – in his view 'the two worst features of life on mental hospital wards' – are mentally and socially demoralising agents. He tried to remedy this situation by giving the majority of his patients productive work and by civilising the conditions of their daily life.

In Belgium the authors visited Gheel. They applauded the basic concept of family care but considered that the patients had the status of recipients of charity – 'as pitiful but inferior beings' – an attitude which they felt would encourage dependency rather than independency. They did not feel that there was a deliberate policy of work or occupational therapy.

In France, they found that social and occupational therapy played an important part in the rehabilitation unit Centre de Traitement et de Re'adaption Sociale Ville – Evrard, created through the initiative of Dr. Paul Sivadon.

"Dr. Sivadon holds that mental breakdown always involves regression to a relatively primitive level of personality integration and he maintains that the character of the raw material used in occupational tasks, the degree of complexity of the tasks and the quality of the social interaction demanded in their performance should each be adapted to the patient's level of regression. Only then, he believes, will the task become meaningful to the patient. As the patient advances to more complex tasks he acquires an increasing sense of responsibility towards his fellows. In this way work therapy helps him to a more mature personality integration."

The re-awakened British interest in work and occupational therapy led to a number of experiments which contributed to the understanding of the needs of long-stay patients and stimulated an optimism in his rehabilitation.

Carstairs, O'Connor and Rawnsley (1956)[5] studied the effects of an industrial workshop on 12 men, aged 26-46 years, who had been continuously in hospital between 4 and 22 years. They anticipated that on entry to the workshop the patients would have a low level of output but that financial reward – geared to output – would act as an incentive to improve and sustain production. Output did improve but the overall production of the group levelled off at between £9 and £10 per week per person, compared with the £24 which 12 young women employed on the same task, would be expected to earn during the same time. Inspection of the pay sheets for the previous three weeks showed that 7 of the 12 men earned only £1 each, yet 4 of them had previously exceeded this figure. It was found that this levelling off was due to the regulations of the National Insurance Act which only permitted a patient to earn £1 per week. As soon as this limit was exceeded he forfeited his residual sickness benefit and became liable to pay 8s. 5d. per week for a self-employed insurance stamp. It was shown that with incentives many long-stay patients are able to achieve normal rates of productivity and that failure to do so may be due to lack of incentive rather than lack of ability.

Regular attendance at the workshop was often accompanied by an 'appreciable improvement' in behaviour. At the start of the experiment 4 patients were under constant surveillance requiring an escort to and from their locked ward, 2 made repeated attempts to escape and 2 were liable to wander off in a disorientated manner. After two months in the workshop no patient was escorted and the 2 escapees were transferred to open wards. One year after commencement 3 patients had been discharged, 1 had absconded, 7 were in open wards and 1 patient was in a closed ward, although still attending the workshop.

Baker (1956)[6] described a similar success following a policy of providing work under factory conditions at Banstead Hospital. The experimental workshop was established by the Medical Research Council and employed 40 women and 20 men who had been in hospital 'for many years'. Within four months of its opening, 3 patients who had been in hospital twenty-four, nineteen and four years had left to take up full-time employment under normal working conditions. Baker felt that the 'improvement in the other patients working in the factory is obvious'. He reported that if patients who were on disturbed wards prior to working were moved to better wards, there was a general increase in pride of appearance and the effects of the institution were lessened. He concluded that a:—

"considerable proportion of long-stay patients shall be discharged and that the large buildings and overcrowded wards which we have known for so many years will become obsolete."

Wittkower and Tendresse (1955)[7], whilst recognising the worth of occupational therapy, felt that its therapeutic value for chronic schizophrenics would be enhanced if its scope were widened. They tested this hypothesis on 12 severely regressed female schizophrenics selected at random and divided into a test and control group. For six months the test group was given the opportunity, in a permissive atmosphere, to play with dirt in order to satisfy their anal needs. At the same time the control group was treated along traditional occupational therapy lines. Comparison at the end of the period showed a 'marked improvement' in the test patients in comparison to the control group. Wittkower and Tendresse claimed that the test patients reached a higher level of psycho-sexual organization with ego maturation and concluded that, no matter how regressed a schizophrenic patient might be, the process is reversable with appropriate occupational therapy.

Wing and Giddens (1959)[8], in attempting to assess the value of Industrial Rehabilitation Units (I.R.U.) in the re-settlement of long-stay patients, conducted an experiment in which 30 long-stay male schizophrenics, aged between 25-45 years, who were thought to require very little nursing care or supervision, were selected to attend an I.R.U. centre. A psychiatrist unconnected with the project was asked to rate the patients and to place them into two categories of severely and moderately disturbed. From these categories 20 patients, 10 severely and 10 moderately disturbed, proceeded to an I.R.U. centre, and 10 acted as the control group and remained in hospital in their normal routine.

At follow-up six months to a year later, of the 10 moderately disturbed patients who went to the I.R.U. centre, 3 were undertaking industrial training courses, 5 others had jobs which seemed to be satisfactory, 1 had left hospital but was living on social security, the remaining patient was still in hospital.

Of the 10 severely ill patients, 2 had obtained employment but were not working at follow-up, 5 had improved sufficiently to be recommended for sheltered employment but had not been placed at follow-up.

Of the controls, only 1 had been discharged from hospital and he was later re-admitted.

This study has value in that it differentiates between the severely and moderately disturbed. The experimental group showed a superiority in disharge and employment over the control group. On this evidence there are advantages to be gained from offering an I.R.U. course to the moderately ill chronic schizophrenic, but the severely handicapped chronic has little chance of re-settlement except through a sheltered workshop.

This last conclusion was supported by Nicholas (1967)[9], who during his attempt to correlate the post-rehabilitation progress of 65 long-stay schizophrenic patients with observations made during rehabilitation at a regional psychiatric unit, found that unless chronic schizophrenic patients function at a sufficiently high level to meet the demands of a rehabilitation programme then their disabilities may well be emphasized by the process.

Wing and Freudenberg (1961)[10] carried out a pilot project on 22 severely ill, long-hospitalised schizophrenics admitted to a hospital workshop for sixteen weeks, two weeks after the withdrawal of medication, to see whether there were changes in workshop output and ward behaviour when conditions in the workshop were experimentally varied.

During the first two weeks the 22 patients were divided into two groups, placed in separate workshops and supervised on alternate days by a male and female supervisor. The patients spent alternate weeks in each workshop. There was no evidence that the change of supervisor or the different room affected production. Following the preliminary two weeks each group was allocated its own supervisor. There was a sharp increase in output whenever social incentives were introduced, and a sharp decrease whenever passive conditions were resumed. Although 11 of the patients accounted for 90 per cent of the production under passive conditions, and for all the improvement resulting from practice, they contributed only 40 per cent of the improvement due to social incentives. Under active supervision various abnormalities of behaviour – immobility, mannerisms and restlessness – decreased, but ward behaviour remained unaffected. This experiment demonstrated that long-stay patients do respond to stimulation and quickly react when it is withdrawn. The authors pressed for further experimentation in order to see whether prolonged and intensive re-education and supervision might reveal further unexpected assets.

Early (1960)[11] developed industrial rehabilitation further by providing employment in factory-like conditions within the institution. The Industrial Therapy Organization (Bristol) was set up in 1958 to prepare patients to enter open employment or industrial training. This scheme was not designed specifically for the chronic patient but its reported success indicates that its value in his rehabilitation requires analysis.

Experiments in Social Therapy

In the rehabilitation of long-stay patients the fundamental question is whether the environment and social events can aid recovery, and if so in what ways.

Barton (1959)[1] felt that 'institutional neurosis' can be treated but to be successful it requires a positive staff attitude, and an enlightened hospital regime, which includes:— the need for the patient to re-establish contact with his family and/or his community; the need for recreational and employment activities – to take up fourteen hours of every day; improving the authoritarian and custodial attitude of the nursing and medical staff; the encouragement of friends and visitors; the patient having his own possessions to help him establish his own identity and individuality; the reduction of drugs which Barton felt in some cases does nothing for the mental state and often produces increasing and harmful drowsiness; the provision of a warm atmosphere in bright optimistic surroundings; encouragement of the patient to take pride in appearance; making the patient aware of the employment and accommodation opportunities outside hospital; and motivating the patient towards seeking his own discharge.

This point of view was supported by Wing and Brown (1961)[12], who designed a study to compare the social treatment of chronic schizophrenics in three mental hospitals. They postulated that if it was true that social routines influence symptoms then it should be possible to demonstrate this phenomenon by comparing clinical condition of patients in different hospitals. The social conditions in the three mental hospitals they examined were very different. They found that where there was emphasis on the care of the long-stay patient, there was least clinical disturbance, most personal freedom, useful occupation and optimism amongst the nursing staff. The opposite held true where reform in the care of the long-stay patient had not progressed beyond custodial lines, there was most clinical disturbance, least personal freedom and little staff optimism.

Myerson (1939)[13] devised a regime to arouse the interest and co-operation of the patient and coined the term 'total push' to describe the technique. In its comprehensiveness it is similar to the description given by Barton. Basically it involved:—

(a) General medical measures – the introduction of vigorous physiotherapy – showers, douches, massages and irradiation in the form of ultra-violet light.

(b) Exercises and games – beginning with simple activities and progressing to those requiring co-ordination and skill.

(c) Improved diet and the supply of vitamins.

(d) Psychological push – by providing clothing which produced pride in appearance; praise, blame and reward of good behaviour to stimulate motivation; teaching and the provision of materials to develop basic artistic skills and craftsmanship; daily entertainment; and by establishment of a dining room.

Myerson claimed that these methods were successful in removing or lessening the degree of social withdrawal and stupor in patients and in boosting the morale of the hospital staff, but there was no mention of recovery.

Sines, Lucero and Kamman (1952)[14] felt that Myerson's treatment was expensive and not suitable for all schizophrenics. With this in mind they attempted to isolate symptoms which would indicate those patients most suitable for the 'total push' type of treatment. At random they selected 54 long-stay regressed schizophrenics and placed them on a six-month 'total push' programme. In addition, during the first six to seven weeks, all patients received a series of twenty electro-convulsive treatments. A control group of matched patients which received electro-convulsive therapy but no social therapy were similarly rated at the end of the six-month period. There was a greater improvement in the 'total push' group than in the control group, but the degree of improvement was related to higher level of original behaviour, shorter length of hospitalisation, and the diagnosis of simple or paranoid schizophrenia or hibephrenia.

Baker and Thorpe (1956)[15] separated out electro-convulsive therapy (E.C.T.) and habit training, and compared the effects of the two methods of treatment on 48 long-stay deteriorated schizophrenic patients placed in three groups of 16. One group was moved to a small ward where an active programme of toilet training, physical exercises, occupational therapy and social activity was instituted, the second group was given a course of E.C.T. but no extra attention, and the third remained as they were. All patients were assessed for one week before the experiment began. The results revealed differences in the effects of habit training compared with E.C.T. There was no change in the control group. In the main, habit training reduced the amount of sleeping in the day, and improved difficulties in conversation, the inability to dress and the level of work. E.C.T. affected specific areas of behaviour and significantly improved feeding difficulties and led to some improvement in retardation. However, the improvement was not at a statistically significant level. Overall habit training seems to have made the greatest improvement but neither regime had an effect on greediness, over-talkativeness, ability to make friendships and relate to one another. Aggressiveness did not improve in the habit training group and worsened in the E.C.T. group.

Phillips and Bell (1957)[16] recognised that most long-stay patients were cared for in wards that represented the backwater in psychiatry. They became interested in the response of long-stay patients to intensive care. For five months a staff group worked closely with 72 long-stay male patients, about 75 per cent of whom had been in hospital continuously for five years or more. In spite of this all patients had maintained a minimum level of social adjustment with little supervision. By the end of the period 26 patients had left hospital and 29 others, although not discharged, no longer required hospital care. The authors stressed the concept of 'social chronicity', rather than clinical chronicity, resulting from the policy of giving indefinite care irrespective of need. They pressed for re-thinking about hospital care and the development of community care for the long-stay patient.

Tourney, Senf, Dunham, Glen and Gottlieb (1960)[17], in an attempt to assess the value of re-socialisation techniques on chronic schizophrenics, selected 40 long-stay patients in a State Hospital and placed half in a research unit for nine months, the remainder acting as control. The goals of the re-socialisation programme were to stimulate inter-personal relationships amongst the patients and encourage the integration of the patient's personality. The ratio of staff to patients in the research unit was 1 to 2, whilst the ratio in the State Hospital was 1 to 20. The experimental group showed sufficient improvement in many of their symptoms to achieve a tenuous type of socialisation. The control group showed no improvement. However, at follow-up at eight and twenty-month intervals after the experiment, the study group had made no further improvement. The cost of the programme was quite prohibitive and prevented its application on a wider scale.

Olsen (S.R.) (1970)[18], in her assessment of the effects of a rehabilitation unit on the social functioning of re-admitted long-stay patients demonstrating a severe degree of social handicap, found "it impossible in view of the variety of stimuli applied to each patient to erect a controlled experiment" and that the value of the inter-patient-staff relationships "was outside the scope of measurement". However, in her evaluation Olsen felt that the unit had value in improving the social functioning in 8 out of the 9 patients she studied.

The Contribution of Drug Therapy

The almost unqualified enthusiasm and support given to the value of occupational and social therapy in improving the social functioning of long-stay patients is not extended to drug therapy, about which a large number of research papers, reflecting the great interest in this field, have produced contradictory findings which are often invalidated by methodological error.

"When we compare the potential usefulness of drugs with our present knowledge of their effects, and the clinical use made of them at the moment, we cannot but note the wide gap which separates expectancy from achievement. Empirical studies there are many, but they are frequently contradictory and bedevilled by many experimental, statistical and methodological errors. Clinical applications show frequent failures to obtain expected results and a general difficulty of predicting the reactions of individuals to the given drugs, to say nothing of the eternal problem of dosage. The present position, therefore, cannot be regarded as satisfactory either from the research or the applied point of view." Eysenck (1957)[19].

This view is shared by Weatherall (1962)[20] who was also sceptical and felt that the value of drugs was a matter of opinion and open to some doubt. In his review of the evidence he concluded that a large number of clinical reports were inadequate and not of value as a firm foundation for knowledge. Very few control studies make use of quantitive methods to estimate the patient's progress or of statistical procedure in this evaluation. The term 'success' is obscure in its definition. Controlled observation by many authors reveals that there are many factors which affect a patient's behaviour besides drugs and that it is "exceptional for improvement not to be reported amongst patients treated with dummy tablets". "Within limits any change in procedure will produce a change in behaviour." Tests reveal discrepancies when control conditions are not adhered to, for example, when the physician knows which drug is the placebo, or when drugs taste or look different. Weatherall concluded that:—

"in spite of the enthusiasm and propaganda, tranquillizing drugs have very little effect. Perhaps their greatest value is in the enthusiasm they arouse. Certainly, their use has been followed by much reduction in the numbers of in-patients in mental hospitals, but this improvement is not uniquely attributable to the use of new drugs."

Horden and Hamilton (1963)[21] in their review of the literature felt that the efficiency of phenothiazine as a treatment method for chronic schizophrenics had not been established and "was no better than the results of 'moral treatment' introduced over a century ago". They felt that the role and part played by phenothiazines in the rehabilitation process had not been established.

Okasha and Tewfik (1964)[22] whilst applying a double-blind controlled trial of haloperidol and placebo on 69 chronic disturbed patients found, as have others, that abrupt withdrawal of heavy doses of phenothiazines produces little change in the behaviour of the patient,

"and it is possible that in many disturbed patients the medication is ineffective and possibly interfering with occupational and social therapy regimes." In many occupational therapy departments, a common sight is to be seen in the afternoons of obese patients fast asleep with their knitting having fallen from their fingers."

The authors concluded,

"Surely much medication is given to our patients to reassure the medical and nursing staff that everything possible is being done."

Barton and Hurst (1966)[23] supported this view in their conclusions following their study of the effectiveness of chlorpromazine on 50 female patients aged between 62-89 years who had been in hospital continuously for 2 to 93 months. "Our trials suggest that about 80 per cent of elderly demented patients are receiving tranquillizers unnecessarily."

Rosati (1964)[24] in an American study, came to the opposite conclusion and in doing so felt that the reason for conflicting reports lay in the lack of standardization in dosage and the variability of duration of treatment, particularly in chronic cases. By prolonging a consistent high dosage of medication in "about 55 male patients", with an averaged stay of seven years, the author was able to discharge 26 patients.

"A follow-up of these 26 cases after about two years in the community indicates that all have been discharged after one year of trial visits."

Five cases relapsed, "all five were due to discontinuance of medication". However, the validity of this study is in doubt as all patients received "intensified ancillary activities" with the purpose of re-educating the patient. No effort was made to measure the effect of this process.

Grygier and Waters (1958)[25] posed a similar question in their study of the effects of chlorpromazine combined with intensive occupational therapy. They found that chlorpromazine was slightly, but significantly, better than placebo after three and six months when combined with occupational therapy. However, they did not assess the value of the drug used on its own.

Post (1963)[26] found that promazine was of value in the management of agitated elderly patients whilst Robinson (1959)[27] who compared the prolonged administration of various drugs against a placebo in a double-blind trial on 84 senile female patients, found no statistically significant improvement associated with the drugs.

Brill and Patton (1957)[28] attributed the population fall of some 500 patients, in comparison to the expected increase of 2,500 in the mental hospitals in New York State in 1956, to the introduction of the tranquilizing drugs, chlorpromazine and reserpine. They repeated their investigation three years later (1959) and found that the depopulation trend had continued. However, in their second study they felt that:—

"it is no longer possible to say that circumstances have remained essentially the same as they were before the use of drug therapy was undertaken; a whole series of progressive changes have occurred; a sweeping program of liberalization of hospital policy has been developed; open hospital techniques, encouragement of admissions other than by judicial certification and the organization of a number of experimental programs have been undertaken."

In view of this the authors found it impossible to separate out the significance of each individual development, including the use of drugs, in the depopulation trend. "What seems certain is that all these elements are mutually interdependent and reinforce each other."

On the presented evidence it appears that, whilst the claim, that the introduction of tranquillizing drugs during the 1950's *coincided* with an increased use of out-patient and community care of the short-stay patient and the reversal of the hospital population trend, has some validity, their efficacy in relation to the care and rehabilitation of the long-stay patient is open to doubt. My own research (1976) [29,30] which examined the personal and social outcome, 2-5 years after discharge of 216 long-stay patients discharged from the North Wales Hospital, Denbigh, confirms that a custodial policy was maintained throughout the first ninety years. After 1938 the clinical and social developments, which continued through until the 1960s, made a dramatic impact upon the custodial trend and the accumulative process was replaced by increasing admission and discharge rates and a falling mortality.

The introduction of new drugs represented a *continuation* and not the *initiation* of a trend begun by the use of the physical methods of treatment, social care and legislative change. Indeed at this hospital at least, the patient population showed a slight rise between 1960-1962, and again in 1964, in spite of their use.

Conclusion

There are no doubts that the papers which describe the use of work and occupational therapy and social therapy in improving the social functioning of psychiatrically disabled persons have important implications for any effort which aims to maintain the mentally disordered in alternative systems to hospital care. However, whilst the majority of reports are optimistic and relate behavioural improvement following experimentation, their findings must, because of the complexities confronting such experiments, be interpreted with some caution. In particular, it is difficult to isolate an individual variable and assess its particular effect on behaviour. In addition it is acknowledged that there are factors which have an effect on the experiment but which cannot be measured with accuracy. For example, the enthusiasm and attitudes that the experimental and non-experimental staff have towards the project; the ripple effect which the project has on other activities or treatment; there is often an absence of matched controls; defining 'improvement' is complex and often relies on subjective opinion or on primitive criteria for evidence; follow-up periods are often short; and the size of the study groups inevitably small.

However, acknowledging the experimental difficulties, the studies, clearly indicate their value and suggest ways in which the return of the long-stay patient to the community might be eased, and social functioning improved once discharge has been effected.

The findings relating to the use of drug therapy in the rehabilitation of the chronic patient remain contradictory. In relation to the long-stay patient there is no evidence to suggest that their use made much impression upon his care within the institution or aided his return to the community. Obviously many more investigations will have to be carried out, not only to establish the efficacy of various drugs in the management of long-stay patients, but also to indicate the inter-relationship of drugs and other treatments available.

References

1. Barton, R., (1959), *Institutional Neurosis,* J. Wright & Sons Ltd., Bristol.
2. Evans, A. E. (1929), Tour of Dutch Mental Hospitals and Clinics, *J. Ment. Sci.,* 75, 192-202.
3. Evans, A. E., (1933), A Tour of Some Mental Hospitals in Western Germany, *J. Ment. Sci., 79, 150-166.*
4. *Carstairs, G. M., Clark, D. J., and O'Connor, N., (1955), Occupational Treatment of Chronic Psychotics, Observations in Holland, Belgium and France, Lancet,* ii. 1025-1030.
5. Carstairs, G. M., O'Connor, N., and Rawnsley, K., (1956), Organization of a Hospital Workshop for Chronic Psychotic Patients, *Brit. J. Prev. Soc. Med.,* 10, 136-140.
6. Baker, A. A., (1956), Factory in a Hospital, *Lancet,* i, 278-279.
7. Whittkower, E. D., and Tendresse, J. D., (1955), Rehabilitation of Chronic Schizophrenics by a New Method of Occupational Therapy, *Brit. J. Med. Psychol.,* 1, XXVIII, 42-47.
8. Wing, J. K., and Giddens, R. G. T., (1959), Industrial Rehabilitation of Male Chronic Schizophrenic Patients, *Lancet,* ii. 505-507.
9. Nicholas, M., (1967a), The Rehabilitation of Long-Stay Schizophrenic Patients, *Brit. J. Psychiat.,* 113, 155-158.
10. Wing, J. K., and Freudenberg, R. K., (1961), The Response of *Severely Ill Chronic Schizophrenic Patients to Social Stimulation, Am. J. Psychiat.,* 118, 311-322.
11. Early, D., (1960), *The Industrial Therapy Organization (Bristol),* A Development of Work in Hospital, *Lancet,* ii, 754-757.
12. Wing, J. K., and Brown, G. W., (1961), Social Treatment of Chronic Schizophrenia, A Comparative Survey of Three Mental Hospitals, *J. Ment. Sci.,* 107, 847.
13. Myerson, A., (1939), Theory and Principles of the 'Total Push' Method in the Treatment of Chronic Schizophrenia, *Am. J. Psychiat.,* 95, 1198-1204.
14. Sines, J. O., Lucero, R. and Kamman, G., (1952), A State Hospital Total Push Program for Regressed Schizophrenics, *J. Clin. Psychol.,* 8, 189-193.
15. Baker, A. A., and Thorpe, J. G., (1956), Deteriorated Psychotic Patients, Their Treatment and its Assessment, *J. Ment. Sci.,* 102.
16. Phillips, F., and Bell, S. M., (1957), A Study of the Transfer of Long-Hospitalized Patients to a Convalescent Villa, *Am. J. Psychiat.,* 114, 4, 344-350.

17. Tourney, G., Senf, R., Dunham, H., Glen, R., and Gottlieb, J., (1960), The Effect of Resocialization Techniques on Chronic Schizophrenic Patients, *Am. J. Psychiat.*, 116, 11, 990-993.

18. Olsen, S. R., (1970), *An Assessment of the Effects of a Rehabilitation Unit on the Social Functioning of Chronic Psychiatric Patients*, available at North Wales Hospital, Denbigh.

19. Eysenck, H. J., (1957), Drugs and Personality: Theory and Methodology, *J. Ment. Sci.*, 103, 430, 119.

20. Weatherall, M., (1962), Tranquillizers, *Brit. Med. J.*, 1, 1219-1224.

21. Horden, A., and Hamilton, M., (1963), Drugs and Moral Treatment, *Brit. J. Psychiat.*, 109, 500-509.

22. Okasha, A., and Tewfik, G. I., (1964), Haloperidol: A Controlled Clinical Trail in Chronic Disturbed Patients, *Brit. J. Psychiat.*, 110, 56-60.

23. Barton, R., and Hurst, L., (1966), Unnecessary Use of Tranquillizers in Elderly Patients, *Brit. J. Psychiat.*, 112, 989-990.

24. Rosati, D., (1964), Prolonged High Dosage Ataractic Medication in Chronic Schizophrenia, *Brit, J. Psychiat.*, 110, 61-63.

25. Grygier, P., and Waters, M. A., (1958), Chlorpromazine Used with an Intensive Occupational Therapy Programme, *A.M.A. Arch. Neurol. and Psychiat.*, 79, 697-705.

26. Post, F., (1963), Mental Confusion in Old Age, *Prescriber's Journal*, 3, 72.

27. Robinson, D. B., (1959), Evaluation of Drugs in Geriatric Patients, *A.M.A. Arch. Gen, Psychiat.*, 1, 41.

28. Brill, H., and Paton, R. E., (1957), Analysis of 1955-56 Population Fall in New York State Mental Hospitals in First Year of Large Scale Use of Tranquillizing Drugs, *Am. J. Psychiat.*, 114, 6, p. 509.

29. Olsen, M. R., (1975), The Non-contribution of Drugs to the Discharge of the Long-Stay Psychiatric Patient, *Social Work Today*, Vol. 5, No. 14.

30. Olsen, M. R. (1976) *The Personal and Social Consequences of the Discharge of the Long-Stay Psychiatric Patient from the North Wales Hospital, Denbigh (1965-66)*, Ph.D. Thesis, University of Wales.

PART THREE

BURDEN ON THE LIVING GROUP

3: Behavioural Problems Demonstrated by Chronic Psychiatric Patients Residing in Non-Institutional and Institutional Living Groups

M. Rolf Olsen

The recognition that mental illness can be interpreted not only according to disturbance and functional impairment but also in terms of the consequent disruptive interactions with others, has led a number of researchers and practitioners to consider the impact of the mentally ill person on his family. However, most of the investigators have been concerned with the influence of the new referral and the short-stay patient, when the effect of behaviour is at its height, and there have been few studies which have considered the burden and anxiety caused by the chronic and discharged long-stay patient to the variety of institutional and non-institutional living groups, including the family, which he may occupy following discharge.

This chapter relates the findings of research[1] carried out in 1969 into the personal and social consequences of 178 chronic patients followed up between 2 and 5 years after discharge from one particular psychiatric hospital.

At the outset it was anticipated that many in the study group, most of whom bore the residues of their condition and the effects of institutionalization, would present difficulties to their living group. In particular, problems in forming relationships, managing their affairs and in maintaining adequate standards of hygiene. It was also thought that a number of patients may have demonstrated odd behaviour or movements, or expressed strange ideas, some of which were tolerated or went unnoticed in the hospital, harmless in themselves but which present a burden to the living group. Therefore, this chapter aims to establish those behavioural and care problems, and any residues of mental illness and long-term institutionalisation, which were present on follow-up. It also seeks to discover how difficulties were described and tolerated; the behaviour which caused the person(s) most concerned with care the most stress; to see if the amount of difficulty, the stress and anxiety it generated and the degree of felt burden varied between the main types of living group; whether it was felt that the patient made a positive contribution to the happiness and well-being of the living group; the number of informants who wished the patient to leave the living group; and to record the informant's estimate of the overall level of social adjustment achieved by each patient.

Method

Each person most responsible for the patient's care was asked to identify and describe the patient's behaviour according to eighty specific variables and any other behaviour not included in the schedule which he/she thought should be incorporated. A total of five other behavioural problems were identified by the informants, making a total of eighty-five.

Informants were asked about each variable in turn and requested to describe the patient's behaviour during the month prior to follow-up, and up to the month prior to follow-up. When the informant(s) considered that the patient's behaviour was abnormal, in relation to any item, he/she was asked whether it caused great stress, some stress or no stress. Each informant was also asked to say whether caring for the patient had been a burden or caused her any anxiety, to state whether she regretted that the patient shared her residence, to judge the patient's level of social adjustment, to indicate whether he had made any contribution to the happiness and well-being of the living group, and to say whether they would like the patient to leave the living group. In addition a count was made of the number of behavioural problems shown by each patient during the month prior to, and up to the month prior to follow-up.

The Total Number and Percentage of Patients Demonstrating Behavioural or Care Problems

A total of 85 behavioural or care problems were demonstrated by two or more of the study group at some time during their stay in the living group occupied on follow-up. Altogether 2,200 problems were scored by the whole of the study group – an average of 12.36 per person.

Table 1 shows that during the month prior to follow-up only 11 (6%) patients were without problems of care or behaviour, 44 (25%) had shown between 1 and 5 problems, 37 (21%) between 6 and 10, 68 (38%) between 11 and 20, and 17 (10%) between 21 and 35. This was an improvement on the score for the period up to a month prior to follow-up when only 7 (4%) patients did not present problems to the caring person, 39 (22%) presented between 1 and 5, 35 (20%) between 6 and 10 and over half (97 = 54%) between 21 and 35.

Table 1 also shows that the ten most frequently recorded behavioural/care problems were:—

(1) that more than half required full (45 = 25%) or some (45 = 25%) (total 90 = 51%), help with the care of their clothes;

(2) that 42 per cent totally (53 = 30%) or partially (22 = 12%), (total 75 = 42%) neglected personal appearance and washing;

(3) that a similar percentage could not ever (68 = 38%) or sometimes (6 = 3%), (total 74 = 42%) be left without supervision;

(4) that more than a third showed no (30 = 17%) or little (37 = 21%), (total 67 = 38%) interest in anything;

(5) had to always (31 = 17%), or sometimes (35 = 20%), (total 66 = 37%) be washed and bathed;

(6) inappropriately talked or laughed out loud (47 = 26%) or muttered to self (18 = 10%), (total 65 = 37%);

(7) required total (42 = 24%) or some (22 = 12%), (total 64 = 36%) supervision of finances;

(8) that 32 per cent were always (36 = 20%) or sometimes (21 = 12%), (total 57 = 32%) extremely slow in carrying out activities;

(9) had no friendships whatsoever (27 = 15%), or made friendships with great difficulty (30 = 17%), (total 57 = 32%);

(10) and that 30 per cent frequently (30 = 17%) or occasionally (24 = 13%), (total 54 = 30%) demonstrated childish behaviour.

Other behavioural problems, confirmed in more than 1 in 5 (36 = 20%) patients were that the patient was usually solitary (52 = 29%), sat or stood in one place for long periods (46 = 26%), was uncooperative or truculent (46 = 26%), was bossy towards others (40 = 22%), was incompatible with others in the living group (39 = 22%), hoards rubbish (39 = 22%), was totally or partially bedridden (39 = 22%), had a physical handicap which presented problems in management (38 = 21%), was generally or frequently demanding (37 = 21%), was encopretic (36 = 20%), or lacked speech (36 = 20%).

The two major conclusions one can draw from this information are firstly that the overall average of 12 behavioural or care problems per person was high compared with that which one would expect reported in a normal living group. Secondly, that the frequent reporting of problems associated with a lack of cleanliness, neglect of clothing, appearance and hygiene and the disinterest, lack of activity and friendships, suggests that the group as a whole were manifesting many of the problems associated with chronic institutionalized psychiatric patients.

Creer (1975)[2] p. 3, describes a similar picture:—

"Although the inability to mix with others was the most frequently reported problem of the withdrawn type several other difficulties of this nature were mentioned by a number of relatives. Some patients spent long hours in total inactivity and were unable to concentrate on any leisure interests. Some hardly spoke, not seeming to hear what others said to them or conversing only in monosyllables. Some were slow in movement or neglected their appearance and cleanliness. There were also patients who presented problems at mealtimes (this often reflecting a general inability to cope with social situations)".

This poverty of personal resources restates the fundamental question of how far these patients were showing signs of a chronic condition and how much of their inability to meet the social expectation was due to the conditioning of years spent in an undemanding custodial environment. Whatever the reason it raises the problem of how far these kinds of inabilities can be alleviated by pre and post-discharge social rehabilitation programmes and by social opportunities designed to reinforce and maintain progress. It also indicates that careful attention should be paid to the needs of long-stay patients currently in hospital, and suggests that preventive procedures should be designed to stop these deprecating forces manifesting themselves in the new chronics.

Behavioural and Care Problems which Caused Stress in Relation to the Living Group on Follow-up

Of the 2,200 scored difficulties 253 (12%) caused great stress, 306 (14%) some stress, and three-quarters (1641 = 75%) no stress. It was also found that behavioural and care problems were interpreted differently by the persons most responsible for care.

This finding, that whilst a behaviour or care problem was similar in a number of living groups, the effect on the caring person in the majority of instances ranged from severe to no stress, supports the conclusion of Hill (1965)[3], that possible stressful events can only be viewed as variables which will be interpreted differently by those involved.

The behaviour or care problems which caused great stress in over 33 per cent of its occurances were: drunkenness (67%), upsetting neighbours (57%), rising too early (55%), refusing to contribute towards keep (50%), damage to property (50%), threatening to harm others (47%), upsetting the living group's routine (47%), refusing to see his doctor (40%), smoking in unsafe places (40%), spitting (40%), inflicting self-injury (40%), showing little interest (38%), and interfering with the activities of others (38%).

It was also found that the percentage of informants who considered that certain behaviour caused stress varied between the three main types of living group: psychiatric hospital (PH), other institutional living groups (OI) and non-institutional living groups (NILG), on follow up.

a) Psychiatric Hospital: (15 patients re-admitted to Hospital).

Whilst the 15 patients in PH scored 205 (100%) behavioural or care problems, in only 3 (1%) instances did the nurse most responsible for care complain that it caused great stress (once because the patient showed little or no interest, once because the patient was unco-operative and truculent and once when a patient inflicted self injury), on only 25 (12%) occasions was some stress felt, and in the great majority of instances (177 = 86%) no stress was experienced.

b) Other Institutional Living Groups: (47 Patients).
Patients in OI recorded 788 behavioural or care problems. In spite of the high average number of difficulties per person the informants claimed that great stress was experienced on only 58 (7%) instances, some stress 69 (9%) times, and no stress in the remaining 661 (84%) occasions.

The behaviour which caused great stress in over 33 per cent of its occurances were:— upsetting neighbours (100%), threatening to harm others (57%), upsetting living group's routine (50%), inappropriate fear (50%), threatening self-injury (50%), damage to property (50%), making unwelcome sexual advances (38%), wandering (33%), persistent restlessness (33%), and upsetting other members of the living group (33%).

c) Non-Institutional Living Groups: (116 Patients).
Although the patients in NILGs were on average less disturbed than those in OI or PH the informants responsible for their care expressed a significantly higher incidence of stress. The patients in NILGs recorded a total of 1,207 problems. Of these the informants felt great stress on 192 (16%) occasions, some stress 212 (18%) times and no stress on 803 (67%) occasions. This difference in the incidence of stress between OI and NILGs reached significance ($x^2 = 73.51$ d.f.l., $P > 0.01$).

The behavioural or care problems in this group which caused great stress in over 33 per cent of its occurrances were:— stuttering (100%), spitting (100%), rising too early (86%), incontinence (83%), drunkenness (67%), damaging property (60%), causing harm to others (55%), refusing to contribute towards keep (50%), refusing to see the doctor (50%), smoking in unsafe places (50%), upsetting the routine of the living group (50%), upsetting neighbours (50%), interference with the activities of others (50%), pilfering (43%), refusing to stay in when should (40%), threatening others (38%), unco-operativeness (38%), and spending long periods in the bathroom (33%).

Behavioural or Care Problem which Caused Most Stress

In addition to being asked to identify all behaviour and care problems and to say which caused stress each informant was asked whether any particular problem stood out as having caused the most stress.

Column 4 of table 2 shows that overall the informants thought that 110 (62%) patients had not presented any problem which caused particular stress, that 68 (38%) had produced 1 of 34 problems which was particularly stressful, and that 2 problems – getting up too early, and interference with the activities of the living group – were nominated most often (6 = 3%) as the behaviour which caused the most stress.

Column 5 of table 2 declares the number presenting particular stress as a percentage of the total number presenting that problem. The findings confirm the view that some problematic behaviour is more likely to cause stress than others, for example, it was found that 2 (50%) of the 4 patients who failed to regularly contribute towards their keep caused the living group most stress, as did persistent early morning rising (46%), interference with the activities of other members of the living group (37.5%), refusing to stay in the residence at times when he should (29%), a reluctance to speak or stuttering (both 25%), and smoking in unsafe places, spitting, and harming self, all 20 per cent.

Table 2, columns 1 to 3, also show that the percentage of informants who considered that certain behaviour caused particular stress varied between the three types of living group.

a) Psychiatric Hospital:

Column 1, shows that only 2 (13%) behavioural problems were thought to have caused the informants in psychiatric hospital particular stress – unco-operative truculent behaviour and a lack of interest.

b) Other Institutional Living Groups:

In comparison, Column 2 shows that nearly half (22 = 47%) of the informants in other institutional care nominated 16 problems which caused them stress. Persistent restleness caused the most stress in 3 (6%) living groups, and unwelcome sexual advances and upset to the living group's routine were each nominated twice (4%).

c) Non-Institutional Living Groups:

Column 3 shows that 44 (38%) of the non-institutional living group informants nominated 23 problems which caused the living group particular stress. Persistent early rising (6 = 5%), interference with the activities of others in the living group (6 = 5%), and regular disturbance at night (3 = 3%) were identified most often.

Whether Caring for the Patient is a Burden or Causes Anxiety

Each informant was asked whether they felt that caring for the patient caused him/her anxiety and whether they found the care to be burdensome.

(i) The Degree of Burden and Anxiety:

Unexpectedly, it was found that 81 per cent of the caring persons experienced no anxiety in looking after the patient, and 87 per cent felt that the patient was not a burden. Overall, 33 (19%) informants considered that the patient caused him/her great (7 = 4%), moderate (9 = 5%), or minimal (17 = 10%) anxiety, and that 24 (13%) found the responsibility a great (4 = 2%), moderate (12 = 7%), or minimal (8 = 4%) burden.

This degree of overall burden appears to be considerably less than that found in other studies.

Brown et al. (1958)[4], in their follow-up study of 229 long-stay patients, assessed the amount of hardship the patient caused the living group on a three-point scale: "severe, moderate and minimal liability". They discovered that "17 per cent were rated severe liability, 28 per cent moderate liability, and 55 per cent minimal or no liability".

Creer (1975)[2], during her study of the relatives of 80 chronic schizophrenics, assessed the degree of impairment in the relative's own health and well-being as a result of caring for the patient. She found that 30 per cent suffered severe impairment, 51 per cent moderate or minimal detriment, and that only 19 per cent suffered no effect. Creer concluded:—

"It was apparent that relatives were suffering quite serious effects on

Table 1

Total Number of Behavioural Problems, presented by Patient during month prior to Follow-up and at any time since joining Living Group, according to Living Group at Follow-up

No. of Behavioural Problems	During month prior to follow-up						At any time since joining Living Group						Total Numbers			
	Psychiatric Hospital		Other Institutional Living Group		Non-Institutional Living Group		Psychiatric Hospital		Other Institutional Living Group		Non-Institutional Living Group		During Last Month Since Joining Living Group		Total Numbers	
	T	%	T	%	T	%	T	%	T	%	T	%	T	%	T	%
0			1	2.13	10	8.62			1	2.13	6	5.17	11	6.18	7	3.93
1					11	9.48					7	6.03	11	6.18	7	3.93
2			1	2.13	7	6.03					11	9.48	8	4.49	11	6.18
3			1	2.13	11	9.48			1	2.13	10	8.62	12	6.74	11	6.18
4			1	2.13	6	5.17			1	2.13	3	2.59	7	3.93	4	2.25
5					6	5.17					6	5.17	6	3.37	6	3.37
6 – 10	7	46.67	7	14.89	23	19.83	6	40.0	6	12.77	23	19.83	37	20.79	35	19.69
11 – 15	4	26.67	12	25.53	21	18.10	4	26.67	14	29.79	24	20.69	37	20.79	42	23.60
16 – 20	2	13.33	13	27.66	16	13.79	1	6.67	10	21.28	12	10.34	31	17.42	23	12.92
21 – 25	2	13.33	6	12.77	3	2.59	3	20.0	6	12.77	10	8.62	11	6.18	19	10.67
26 – 30			3	6.38	2	1.72	1	6.67	6	12.77	3	2.59	5	2.81	10	5.62
31 – 35			2	4.26					2	4.26	1	0.86	2	1.12	3	1.69
Total	15	100.	47	100.	116	100.	15	100.	47	100.	116	100.	178	100.	178	100.

Table 2
The Behavioural and Care Problems Nominated by the Informant as causing Particular Stress in Relation to Living Group on Follow-up

Behaviour	Column 1 Psychiatric Hospital		Column 2 Other Institutional Living Group		Column 3 Non-Institutional Living Group		Column 4 Total Number		Column 5 Percentage of Total No. Demonstrating Problem
	T	%	T	%	T	%	T	%	%
Little or No Interest	1	6.67			4	1.72	5	2.81	7.46
Difficulty in Making Friends					1	0.86	1	0.56	1.75
Solitariness					1	0.86	1	0.56	1.92
Housebound					2	1.72	2	1.12	10.53
Refuses to Stay In					2	1.72	2	1.12	28.57
Incompatibility with Living Group					2	1.72	2	1.12	5.13
Refuses to Contribute Towards Keep					2	1.72	2	1.12	50.0
Difficult to Get Out of Bed					1	0.86	1	0.56	3.03
Gets Up Too Early					6	5.17	6	3.37	46.15
Disturbed Behaviour at Night					3	2.59	3	1.69	13.64
Uncooperative and Truculent Behaviour	1	6.67	1	2.13			2	1.12	4.35
Smokes in Unsafe Places			1	2.13	1	0.86	2	1.12	20.0
Neglects Appearance			1	2.13			1	0.56	1.33
Over-Concerned with Cleanliness					2	1.72	2	1.12	13.33
Urinary Incontinence					2	1.72	2	1.12	7.14
Encropresis			1	2.13	2	1.72	3	1.69	8.33
Preoccupation with bowels			1	2.13			1	0.56	8.33
Makes Unwelcome Sexual Advances			2	4.26			2	1.12	18.18
Slowness in Carrying Out Activities					1	0.86	1	0.56	1.75
Sits or Stands in One Place for Long Periods					1	0.86	1	0.56	2.17
Persistent Restlessness			3	6.38	1	0.86	4	2.25	11.76
Muteness or Silence					2	1.72	2	1.12	25.0
Overtalkative					1	0.86	1	0.56	3.85
Stuttering					1	0.86	1	0.56	25.0
Interfers with Activities of Others					6	5.17	6	3.37	37.5
Upsets Living Group's Routine			2	4.26			2	1.12	13.33
Spitting			1	2.13			1	0.56	20.0
Hoards Rubbish			1	2.13			1	0.56	2.56
Physical Harm to Others			1	2.13			1	0.56	4.55
Threatened Harm to Others			1	2.13			1	0.56	6.67
Harm to Self			1	2.13			1	0.56	20.0
Talks or Laughs to Self			3	6.38			3	1.69	4.63
Inappropriate Fear of Ordinary Matters			1	2.13			1	0.56	7.69
Grimaces			1	2.13			1	0.56	3.70
Nil	13	86.67	25	53.19	72	62.07	110	61.80	
Total	15	100.	47	100.	116	100.	178	100.	100.

their health and general well-being because of their problems with the patient" (p. 4).

(ii) Variation Between the Primary Living Groups:

It was found that the amount of felt anxiety and burden varied between the living groups (tables 3-4).

(a) Psychiatric Hospital: As was expected the incidence of anxiety and burden was lowest in psychiatric hospital. Only 1 (7%) informant considered that the care caused moderate anxiety and none thought that the care was a burden.

(b) Other Institutional Care: It was interesting to find that of the 3 types of living group the staffs in other institutions expressed the greatest amount of anxiety. Twelve (26%) considered that the care caused them great (1 = 2%), moderate (2 = 4%), or minimal (9 = 9%) anxiety, and 4 (9%) found the care to be a great (1 = 2%), or moderate (3 = 6%) burden.

(c) Non-Institutional Care: Twenty (17%) of those in non-institutional living groups thought that the care caused them great (6 = 5%), moderate (6 = 5%), moderate (6 = 5%), or minimal (8 = 7%) anxiety, and the highest percentage (20 = 17%) felt that the care was a great (3 = 3%), moderate (9 = 8%), or minimal (8 = 7%) burden.

The difference between the number in OI and NILGs who felt that caring for the patient was a burden or caused anxiety does not reach the desired level of statistical significance.

Table 3

Whether Caring For The Patient Causes Anxiety, According To The Living Group On Follow-Up

Degree of Anxiety	Psychiatric Hospital		Other Institutional Living Group		Non-Institutional Living Group		Total Number	
	T	%	T	%	T	%	T	%
Great Anxiety			1	2.13	6	5.17	7	3.93
Moderate Anxiety	1	6.67	2	4.26	6	5.17	9	5.06
Minimal Anxiety			9	19.15	8	6.90	17	9.55
No Anxiety	14	93.33	35	74.47	96	82.76	145	81.46
Total	15	100.	47	100.	116	100.	178	100.

Table 4

Whether Informant Feels That Caring For The Patient Is A Burden, According To Living Group On Follow-Up

Degree of Burden	Psychiatric Hospital		Other Institutional Living Group		Non-Institutional Living Group		Total Number	
	T	%	T	%	T	%	T	%
Great Burden			1	2.13	3	2.59	4	2.25
Moderate Burden			3	6.38	9	7.76	12	6.74
Minimal Burden					8	6.90	8	4.49
No Burden	15	100.	43	91.49	96	82.76	154	86.52
Total	15	100.	47	100.	116	100.	178	100.

Whether Patient Makes A Positive Contribution To The Happiness And Well-Being Of The Living Group

There is a conspicuous lack of positive thinking about the effect of the discharged long-stay patient on his living group in the literature which I have examined, and I know of no study which has assessed the worth of the patient in terms of the happiness he gives or the contribution he makes to his personal relationships and the well-being of his living group. This suggests that we anticipate that patients will continue to occupy negative recipient roles, perform inadequately and make no contribution to his living situation.

To test this assumption I asked each person(s) most concerned with the patient's care to consider whether the patient made a positive contribution to the living group and if so to estimate the amount on a three-point scale.

Overall, it was considered that 101 (56%) patients made either a great (38 = 21%), moderate (34 = 19%), or minimal (29 = 16%) contribution to, and that 77 (43%) played no part, in the happiness and well-being of the living group.

The ways in which patients were thought to contribute were as different as the patients themselves. They varied from the devoted nursing care willingly given by one patient single-handed to his brother who became chronically sick after the patient was discharged from hospital, to the 'marital bliss' given by one female to her new husband, to every day concern, support and companionship.

The opinion about whether the patient contributed varied significantly between living groups and improved the further one moved from the psychiatric setting. For example, only 3 (20%) of those in psychiatric hospital were thought to have positively contributed, compared to 18 (38%) of those resident in other institutions and 80 (60%) of those living in non-institutional living groups (table 5). The difference between the number who were thought to make a contribution in OI and NILG reaches statistical significance ($x^2 =$ 13.12, d.f.l, p $<$ 0.01).

The reasons for this variation may indicate a number of factors, including the possibility that the NILGs were caring for the least disturbed and/or handicapped who were therefore the most able to contribute; it may reflect different levels of expectation by the informants; or it might indicate support for the view that patients in institutions are cared for and are not placed in a position where they are able and/or expected to contribute.

Table 5

Whether Patient Makes A Positive Contribution To Happiness And Well-Being Of Living Group, According To The Living Group On Follow-Up

Level of Contribution	Psychiatric Hospital		Other Institutional Living Group		Non-Institutional Living Group		Total Number	
	T	%	T	%	T	%	T	%
Great	1	6.67	2	4.26	35	30.17	38	21.35
Moderate	1	6.67	9	19.15	24	20.69	34	19.10
Minimal	1	6.67	7	14.89	21	18.10	29	16.29
Nil	12	80.0	29	61.70	36	31.03	77	43.23
Total	15	100.	47	100.	116	100.	178	100.

Number Whom It Was Thought Should Live Elsewhere

(i) Number who Regret Patient Sharing Accommodation:

In only 11 (6%) instances, all in non-institutional living groups, did the informant regret agreeing to the patient sharing their accommodation (table 6).

(ii) Number who Wish Patient to Live Elsewhere:

However, it was thought by the informants that 22 (12%) patients were wrongly placed and should be accommodated elsewhere (table 7).

Of the 15 patients in psychiatric hospital, the informants thought that 6

(40%) should reside elsewhere – 3 in an approved boarding-house, 1 in a welfare home, and 2 on another ward in the hospital. It was thought that only 1 (2%) of the 47 patients in other institutions was wrongly placed and that she should be admitted to a general hospital. Non-institutional living group informants thought that 15 (13%) patients should be transferred – 6 to a welfare home, 3 to psychiatric hospital, and 2 each to the care of parents, siblings, or a local authority hostel. It should be pointed out that the motive for recommending that the patient be cared for elsewhere was not always one of rejection but often because it was thought to be in the patient's interests.

Table 6

Whether Informant Regrets Agreeing To Patient Sharing Accommodation, According To Living Group On Follow-Up

Regrets Patient Sharing	Psychiatric Hospital		Other Institutional Living Group		Non-Institutional Living Group		Total Number	
	T	%	T	%	T	%	T	%
Yes	0	—	0	—	11	10.48	11	6.18
No	15	100.	47	100.	105	90.52	167	93.82
Total	15	100.	47	100.	116	100.	178	100.

Table 7

Whether Informant Considers That Patient Should Leave The Living Group According To Living Group On Follow-Up

Informant's Opinion	Psychiatric Hospital		Other Institutional Living Group		Non-Institutional Living Group		Total Number	
	T	%	T	%	T	%	T	%
Yes	6	40.0	1	2.13	15	12.93	22	12.36
No	9	60.0	46	97.87	101	87.07	156	87.64
Total	15	100.	47	100.	116	100.	178	100.

Table 8

**If Informant Considers That Patient Should Leave The Living Group –
Opinion As To Where Patient Should Reside, According To Living Group
On Follow-Up**

Alternative Residence	Psychiatric Hospital		Other Institutional Living Group		Non-Institutional Living Group		Total	Number
	T	%	T	%	T	%	T	%
Parental Home					2	13.33	2	9.09
Sibling's Home					2		2	9.09
Approved Boarding House	3	50.0					3	13.64
Welfare Home	1	16.67			6	40.0	7	31.82
Return to Psychiatric Hospital					3	20.0	3	13.64
General Hospital			1	100.			1	4.55
Hostel					2	13.33	2	9.09
Another Psychiatric Ward	2	33.33					2	9.09
Total	6	100.	1	100.	15	100:	22	100.

The Level of Social Adjustment: The Informant's Opinion

To gain a global view of the informant's opinion of the patient's overall progress each informant was asked to consider the patient's overall progress during the follow-up period and indicate the level of social adjustment on a five-point scale (table 9).

Overall, it was considered that two-thirds (121= 68%) had made a very good (44%) to good (24%) adjustment, 29 (16%) a moderate, and 28 (16%) poor to very poor adjustment.

As with the opinion as to whether the patient had made a positive contribution to the living group it was found that the level of adjustment was thought to be greater the further one moved from a psychiatric setting. Only 1 (7%) patient in psychiatric hospital was thought to have made a good adjustment, for 6 (40%) it was thought that their adjustment was moderate, and for 8 (53%) poor to very poor. Over half (26 = 55%) of those in other institutional groups were regarded as having made a very good to good adjustment, 9 (19%) moderate, and 12 (26%) a poor to very poor adjustment. On the other hand, over three-quarters of those (94=81%) in non-institutional living groups were thought to have made a very good to good adjustment, 14 (12%) moderate, and only 8 (7%) were thought to have made a poor adjustment. The difference between the number who were thought to have made a very good to good adjustment in OI and NILGs reached statistical significance ($x^2 = 11.39$, d.f.l., $p < 0.01$).

Again this variation between living groups is subject to a number of factors, including the probability that the most disturbed were cared for in institutions and different levels of conceptualization and expectation amongst the informants.

Table 9

Informant's Assessment Of The Patient's Overall Social Adjustment, According To Living Group On Follow-Up

Level of Social Adjustment	Psychiatric Hospital		Institutional Living Group		Other Non-Institutional Living Group		Total Number	
	T	%	T	%	T	%	T	%
Very Good	—		10	21.28	69	59.48	79	44.38
Good	1	6.67	16	34.04	25	21.55	42	23.60
Moderate	6	40.0	9	19.15	14	12.07	29	16.29
Poor	6	40.0	10	21.28	8	6.90	24	13.48
Very Poor	2	13.33	2	4.26	—		4	2.25
Total	15	100.	47	100.	116	100.	178	100.

References

1. Olsen, M. R. (1976), *The Personal and Social Consequences of the Discharge of the Long-stay Psychiatric Patient from the North Wales Hospital, Denbigh,* PhD Thesis, Univ. of Wales.
2. Creer, C. (1975), Living with Schizophrenia, *Social Work Today,* Vol. 6, No. 1, 2-7.
3. Hill, R., 'Generic Features of Families Under Stress', *Crisis Intervention,* ed. Parad, H. J., Family Service Association of America, 1965 (first published in *Social Casework,* Vol. XXXIX, Nos. 2-3, 1958).
4. Brown, G. W., Carstairs, G. M. & Topping, G. (1958), 'Post-Mental Hospital Adjustment of Chronic Mental Patients', *Lancet,* ii, 685-689.

PART FOUR

HOSTEL CARE

4: "Somewhere to Live": A Pilot Study of Hostel Care

Sheila Hewett

Introduction

In 1973 a pilot study of residential care in the community for people who had experienced psychiatric illness and its treatment in hospital, was planned and carried out by members of the Medical Research Council Social Psychiatry Unit. One of its most important purposes was to test and, if necessary, modify measures used in previous studies of the environments provided by hostels, so that the nature of the care and support afforded by them could be more adequately described. This was seen as an essential step towards the evaluation of hostel care in comparison with alternative living environments such as group homes, sheltered housing and lodging schemes, which was planned as a second stage of the study. The whole was intended to provide useful information for those planning and setting up such community based support. This paper examines in detail one of the measures tested and discusses ways in which acceptance or rejection of the assumptions upon which the measure is based can influence provision. It also shows the ways in which this particular measure was inadequate.

The conviction that it is inappropriate for large numbers of people with psychiatric disorders to live in hospitals for long periods of time, has been growing in strength for some twenty years. During that time, evidence has accumulated that hospital regimes could prove harmful rather than therapeutic and various attempts have been made to reduce the numbers of people having long hospital admissions and to provide more suitable environments in which they might recover from the effects of their disorders both inside the hospitals and in other accommodation. Clark and Cooper (1960) described an early experiment to set up what they called a "half-way" hostel which exemplified the thinking about mental after-care outside hospital current at that time. The hostel was to be half-way between hospital and ordinary living environments and it would provide a rehabilitation programme while at the same time easing the residents towards independent living. The rehabilitation process would have begun in hospital, would continue in the hostel and would ensure a continual flow of residents from hospital, through the hostel and out into the ordinary world. It was thought that six months would be ample time for the hostel to do its work and in many of the first hostels, this time limit was set.

However, it soon became apparent that it was difficult to select patients who were capable of reaching independence within this period of time. Hostels were left with empty places and at the same time residents who were accepted tended to stay for much longer than the prescribed time. The hostel movement began to lose momentum and during the late 1960s and early 1970s several attempts were made to clarify their problems and offer solutions (Durkin, 1971; Fletcher, 1970; Mounteney 1965, 1968).

An earlier analysis of the environmental characteristics of hospital wards had been carried out (Wing and Brown, 1970) showing that the amount of freedom allowed to schizophrenic patients and the amount of social stimulation provided for them, aided or hindered their recovery. Understimulating social environments and unnecessary restrictions on personal liberty appeared to increase their social withdrawal and lack of interest in life. Improvements in the environments led to reduction of these adverse concomitants of mental disorder.

Using Wing and Brown's approach, Apte (1968) undertook an analysis of the environments of a national sample of hostels in terms of the degree to which they were "restrictive" or "permissive" and tested the hypothesis that "permissive" hostel environments would be more conducive to the growth of independence in residents. He found this hypothesis upheld, since more people tended to leave the "permissive" hostel after a short stay than was the case in "restictive" hostels. The hostels where the majority of residents stayed a short time he termed "transitional" and the others "non-transitional" or "long-stay". He found that 40% of hostel residents were long-stay and mentioned a long list of problems which any critic would recognise as characteristic of poor mental hospitals. He commented: "Without a clarification of purpose, the halfway house could turn into a diffuse and aimless institution, similar to the *workhouse* of former years." Fletcher (op. cit.) put it like this: "Some way must be found to avoid the development of new chronic wards; isolated and forgotten in the middle of the community as surely as they were at the back of the asylum." Mountney (op. cit.) warned that transitional hostels could become, "almost a replica of the worst aspects of old institution life but at almost twice the cost". So far, there has been *no* encouraging study of hostels for the adult mentally ill and the contrast with the earlier optimistic reports about techniques adopted in the best mental hospitals is very striking (Barton, 1959; Clark, 1964; Freudenberg, 1967).

In 1973, in a climate of opinion which was increasingly in favour of reducing the numbers of people in psychiatric hospitals and when "community care" was the watchword, a pilot study was carried out by the Medical Research Council Social Psychiatry Unit (Hewett, Ryan and Wing, 1975; Ryan and Hewett, 1976) to devise and test measures which could evaluate the different kinds of community care which had been developing – not only hostels but group homes, sheltered lodgings schemes, bed-sitting-room schemes and anything else that might come to light. In the event, there were only hostels available for study since all residents from the three London boroughs, (Lambeth, Lewisham and Southwark) who formed the pilot study population, were in hostels. (Six people living in unsupervised bed-sitting rooms were also seen but studied separately.)

The three local authorities were unstinting in the help and co-operation they gave, providing the names and hostel addresses of all the mentally ill people aged 16-65 who were receiving financial support from them while living in 25 hostels. Ninety people in all were referred by the three boroughs but it was possible to visit only 63 of them, the rest being so geographically scattered (from Bournemouth to Ipswich) that it was not practicable to include them.

There was a further problem. The majority of the people referred to the research team were living in hostels run by voluntary bodies and it had been hoped that this would be a study of local authority provision. There was actually only one local authority hostel among the 25 available for study. The residents of this hostel were drawn from other boroughs as well as from Lambeth, Lewisham and Southwark but it was agreed by these boroughs that their residents could be approached and thirteen of their residents were eventually included in the study. Finally 76 people living in 10 hostels formed our main pilot study sample, nine of them run by four voluntary bodies[1] who were as generous with their help as were the local authorities.

The main findings of this pilot study and the methods of data-collection have been reported elsewhere (Hewett, Ryan and Wing op. cit.). Apte's "Hospital/Hostel Practices Profile" was included in the measures used and it is intended here to give detailed consideration to Apte's concepts of "restrictiveness" and "permissiveness" in terms of their meaning for hostel residents. It was one of the aims of the research team to refine this measure if possible before taking the study a stage further, to include the other kinds of provision mentioned above.

Much of the discussion which follows turns on differences and similarities between Apte's findings and our own and it is therefore important to point out some methodological differences between the two studies.

The most important difference concerns sampling and details of Apte's samples are given in an appendix. Apte obtained data about the total populations of a nation-wide sample of hostels. We sampled not hostels, but people, and confined our studies to Southern England. With one exception, we studied only a few individuals in each hostel environment and can say nothing about the remainder of the residents in these hostels. Nor could we follow Apte's practice of defining "transitional" or "long-stay" hostels in terms of the numbers of residents who have in fact stayed one year or longer. Apte states: "When at least half the residents (50% or more) leave the hostel within one year (excluding those who stay for one week or less and those who return to the hospital) the hostel will be considered a transitional hostel." He does not give the exact time limit during which this criterion was applied.

We define hostels in terms of the intentions of their sponsoring bodies. They are therefore divided into two types: (1) short-stay or rehabilitation hostels, where residents are not expected to make a permanent home (many residents may in fact have lived there several years but the intention of the hostel is still that they *should* leave), and (2) those hostels that are set up specifically to provide permanent or indefinite care.

Because of the fragmented nature of Apte's study and difficulty in discovering which of his several samples his figures refer to, it is virtually impossible to make direct comparisons between his data and our own, either on the hostel environments or on the residents. We have used his Hostel/Hospital Practices Profile in eight of the hostels we visited, including both long and short stay. Apte used the scale only on the 25 hostels which he had defined as short-stay ("transitional") in practice.

We found that the majority of the residents from the London boroughs were living in "permissive" environments as defined by Apte's criteria, even those in homes intended to be long-stay. Apte made no analysis of the environment in long-stay or "non-transitional" hostels. Of those in our sample living in "short-stay" permissive hostels, 65% had stayed for more than one year, 43% for more than two years. We must emphasize that these percentages refer to our sampled residents, not to the total populations of the hostels, but in the one short-stay hostel where we saw the total population, the proportions were very similar. We did not, therefore, find the relationship suggested by Apte between short stay of residents and "permissiveness" of the environment. However, we think it is still important to discuss the meaning of the terms "permissive" and "restrictive" as defined by Apte's measure.

As far as the populations of the two studies are concerned, in spite of the difficulties in making comparisons it can be said with some certainty that in both studies the majority of the residents had either never married or were currently divorced, separated or widowed. More than half were over 45 years old and had similar histories of long or frequent admissions to hospital. Both groups tended to be socially isolated. The greatest difference between these populations, separated by 10 years in time, appears to lie in the fact that 80% of our sample were in full-time open employment with only 3% totally unoccupied, while 46% of the 851 people who passed through Apte's 25 transitional hostels were unemployed while they were in the hostels. However, when remaining in employment is a condition of stay in the hostel, as it is in the short-stay hostels in our study, it is hardly surprising to find that residents are employed. Apte states that in the hostels he saw, there was a strong emphasis on the importance of getting a job but that when the "outcome" of hostel stay was studied for 780 of the 1,192 first admissions that constituted his 1963 sample, (see appendix), he found that 40% or more of those under age 60 still had no job when they left the hostel. In our own study, those not successful in getting work may well have had to leave the hostels, either to go back to hospital, or to live elsewhere, where the work expectation was less strictly applied, thus leaving behind a group of people who had achieved the main aim of rehabilitation yet still remained in a sheltered environment.

The degree to which residents were "sheltered" is partly revealed in the discussion of the Hospital/Hostel Practices Profile which follows.

The Hospital/Hostel Practices Profile

The Profile consists of 65 statements regarding day to day practices within the hostel or hospital ward. Wardens or nursing staff give responses that indicate whether or not these practices are carried out, indicating to the investigator those activities of patients or residents which are subject to restriction. Eight of the ten hostel wardens we contacted completed the Profile and their replies are summarised below.

In our personal interviews with residents we asked them to tell us about the same practices (but not in response to the Profile statements) and their answers corroborated the wardens' replies.

Summary of frequency of restrictive scores

1. Items never scored as "restrictive" practices for any hostel

Item No.		(Answer which would have been "restrictive")
3.	Residents need passes or permission to stay out after 7 p.m.	YES
5.	Residents may stay out later than 10 p.m. during the week	NO
6.	Residents may stay out later than 11 p.m. during the week	NO
8.	Residents are expected to be in bed by 10 p.m.	YES
9.	Residents are expected to be in bed by 11 p.m.	YES
11.	Residents may go out alone in the evenings	NO
14.	There are precautions e.g. locked doors, to prevent residents leaving	YES
15.	Residents may go out for alcoholic beverages in the evening	NO
19.	Residents may make a cup of tea	NO
23.	Bathrooms are private	NO
24.	Toilets are private	NO
25.	Bathing is supervised	YES
32.	There are required items of dress	YES
35.	There are restrictions on the display of personal belongings	YES
36.	Residents' belongings are catalogued by staff	YES
37.	Residents' belongings are checked for "forbidden" items	YES
41.	Residents may bath or shower when they like	NO
46. 47.	Visitors have to leave the hostel by 9 p.m.	YES
51.	Residents do their own personal laundry	NO
52.	Residents take full responsibility for their possessions	NO

53.	Residents may retain all of their money	NO
54.	Residents may possess matches or lighters	NO
55.	Residents may possess razors	NO
56.	Residents make their own beds	NO

2. Items scored as "restrictive" practices for one to four hostels

Item No.		Number of hostels using restriction
2.	Residents must be up by a certain time on weekdays, even when not in work	4
4.	Front door is locked at midnight. Residents do not have a key	2
7.	Residents may not stay out as late as they choose at night	1
10.	Residents must be in bed by midnight	1
12.	Staff check that residents are in at night	4
13.	Staff check that residents are in bed at night	2
17.	There is no choice of beverages at meals	1
20.	Residents cannot make a snack between meals	2
21.	No spirits may be brought into the hostel	3
22.	No beer may be brought into the hostel	2
28.	No locked drawer or cupboard for residents' possessions	2
29.	Residents are protected from harm in some way (usually only by staff controlling and storing medicines)	3
30.	Residents are weighed on admission	1
31.	Residents are weighed routinely/periodically	2
33.	Some items of dress are required in the evening	1
34.	No vehicles may be parked by residents	1
38.	Belongings are checked at intervals	1
39.	Residents may not rest on their beds during the day	1
40.	Residents may not watch T.V. after 11 p.m.	1

49.) 50.)	Members of the opposite sex are not allowed in bedrooms either before or after 8 p.m.	3
59.) 60.)	A hairdresser comes to the hostel	2
64.	The psychiatrist visits the hostel	2
63.	Residents must consult staff before visiting their G.P.	?

3. Items scored as "restrictive" practices for five or more hostels

Item No.		*Number of hostels using restriction*
1.	Although residents may go away freely at week-ends hostels like to know where they have gone	8
16.	No choice of main dishes at mealtimes	5
18.	Residents have no say in planning the menu (but wardens say personal preferences are taken into account)	5
26.	Residents' rooms can be entered at any time	7
27.	Residents do not have keys to their rooms	8
42.	Residents may not smoke in bedrooms	5
43.	Restrictions on visiting, of some kind, exist	5
57.) 58.)	Staff call residents or check that they are up in the morning	6
61.) 62.)	Staff retain some control of medicines, although this may be varied to suit individual residents	7
65.	There is no regular meeting of residents and staff	5

Twenty-six of the 65 items on the Profile were never used restrictively by any hostel. Ten others were used only once. Items which were used by five or more hostels out of the eight who completed the Profile are of most interest, since they appear to be important to the majority of hostel wardens.

Whether these items are restrictive in a negative sense only is open to discussion. In discussion with wardens as they completed the Profile it became clear that there was usually a rationale common to all the hostels for the items scored. Thus:

Item 1. People were free to go away at week-ends but in seven out of eight hostels staff liked to know an address which could be contacted if people failed to return. The eighth explained that in case of fire, it was useful to know who was in the hostel. The other reason for knowing who was present or away was the need to know the numbers requiring meals. This does not seem unreasonable. Small hotels must have similar 'restrictions' and even in normal families mothers like to know who is going to be in for dinner.

Items 16 and 18. Allowing no choice in food makes it easier for staff to provide reasonable meals on a low budget. Few residents complained about food.

Items 26 and 27. These seemed to the research team to constitute a definite restriction on privacy, particularly in the local authority hostel where everyone had a single room and a key was available. Again the fear of fire was offered as an explanation and the fear that people might harm themselves (by self poisoning mainly) behind locked doors. One hostel emphasised the desire to create a family atmosphere (doors are not locked in family homes; on the other hand unrelated adults do not usually enter each others' bedrooms without knocking) and in those where rooms were shared by several people, privacy was a problem anyway. However, only twelve of the 34 people sharing bedrooms with one or two other people said they would have preferred to have their own rooms and 75% of the whole sample felt that there was enough privacy, in spite of the fact that 33% of them said that not everyone asked for permission to come in when they were in their rooms. Obviously staff, including cleaners, could enter at any time when residents were away from the hostel. The research team was frequently shown the rooms both when residents were in them and when they were not but this was also true of the six bedsitters in the Housing Association house, where all the rooms had Yale locks but the rent-collector had keys to them all. It seems likely that this reflects the feeling of the staff that residents are not yet fully capable of complete autonomy and that staff would feel responsible and blame themselves if accidents did happen. Whatever the explanation, few residents appeared to resent it. Perhaps it is a small price to pay for the other advantages of hostel living compared with available alternatives.

Item 42. The realistic fear of fire in old, converted property accounts for restrictions on smoking in bedrooms. There was no restriction in the purpose-built Local Authority hostel because, although fire was equally feared here, it was far less likely to spread quickly and fire safety arrangements were built in.

Item 43. The restrictions on visitors were very moderate, mostly requiring visitors to leave the hostel by 11 p.m. or a little later and were imposed out of consideration for all residents. Since most people had to be up early for work, the restriction did not seem to be unreasonable.

Items 57 and 58. Where getting to work on time is important if one is to keep one's job, it seems practical for staff to ensure that people are up in the morning. Many working men in ordinary families are called in the morning by their wives and *vice versa*.

Items 61 and 62. Supervision of medicines, varied in degree to meet the requirements of individuals, was carried out in seven of the eight hostels where the scales were completed. The warden of the eighth gave contradictory replies, claiming no restriction on the Apte scale but stating at interview that it was inconvenient for staff to share the evening meal with residents because medicines were being given out.

More than three-quarters of the sample had a diagnosis of schizophrenia and only six residents were taking no psychotropic drugs at all. Sixty-six per cent were having major tranquillising drugs by mouth and it is well-known that such people may stop taking their drugs when they feel well. Sixty-three per cent of residents felt that they had no psychiatric disability or illness at the time of interview. If they stopped taking their drugs the chance of relapse and re-admission to hospital would be increased. Perhaps staff were, once more, being realistic in attempting to ensure that drugs were taken, but if this is so, it raises the question of what would happen when residents moved out to live alone. Would they continue to take medication or would they stop and then relapse or lose their jobs, or both? One solution is to administer long-acting drugs by injection and 22% of the hostel residents were receiving fluphenazine injections.

Item 65. There appears, on the face of it, to be no justification for the absence of a regular meeting whereby residents may participate in some way in the running of the hostel. Four of the hostels having no meeting were run by a voluntary body which exercised strong direction from head office and the same was true of the fifth although it was run by a different voluntary body.

Discussion

According to scores on the Apte Profile, the hostels we saw retained very few institutional characteristics. Those retained by the majority of hostels could be seen as having positive value for the residents as well as administrative convenience for the staff. Looked at from another point of view, they can be seen as providing the kind of interest and concern that family members give to one another. The parents or spouse, for example, of a person suffering from schizophrenia and living at home, would no doubt try to make sure that he took his medicine and would be anxious if he were away from home for several days without their knowing where he had gone or when he might return. Similarly in many families meals are produced by the mother and the other adults in the family do not have choices of menu on every occasion. It would be misleading to suppose that complete freedom of choice or of action for every individual is customarily found in any group of people living together. Such freedom is "enjoyed" only by those living alone.

If the retention of such practices is instrumental in helping residents to function well and stay in their jobs, should they not be seen as "enabling" rather than "restrictive" practices? Total absence of control may mean total absence of support. Hostels, after all, are meant to provide more than just shelter. Apte himself stated that two hostels had had to close because they were "too permissive" but he did not define what he meant by this.

However, the problem arises that in the rehabilitation hostels the aim is that residents should come to be able to manage without this degree of "family type" day-to-day support and interest and leave the hostel. Mountney (op. cit.), Fletcher (op. cit.) and Durkin (op. cit.) all make the distinction between "rehabilitative" and "compensatory" hostels, putting forward the view that the latter should only be for those who have not been successfully "rehabilitated". The possibility that a working group may continue to need a compensatory environment is not considered.

Apte differs from the present author in that he sees no positive value in the retention of any "restrictive" practices, not even in the supervision of medicines. He sees the ability to control one's own medication as one of the main indications that successful rehabilitation has taken place. When he asked hostel wardens to place the functions of the hostel in rank order of importance, that of control of medication was most frequently placed last (of least importance), although the wardens reported that they spent a considerable amount of time and energy on this "unimportant" task.

In Apte's, as in the present study, a high proportion of residents were taking medication for their psychiatric condition and Apte sees this as "indicative of the degree to which the residents were still placed in the sick role". The long term taking of medicine, need not imply that the taker is thereby placed in the sick role. On the contrary, such medication may be instrumental in helping him to stay out of it. A parallel in physical medicine would be the large number of people with heart conditions, who take digoxin indefinitely but who are not thereby placed in the sick role and who continue to work and to function normally in other ways as well. There may be a danger in assuming that mentally ill people should dispense entirely with supervision of their medication. In discussing the creation of "normalised" living environments for people who are mentally retarded, Gunzburg (1973) has pointed out that it is "quite unacceptable that all types of unsupportive and positively adverse factors are admitted to a so-called normalized environment simply because they are encountered in the ordinary community." There are parallels for those who are mentally ill.

Apte has attributed the persistence of many "restrictive" practices to the fact that wardens had had many years working in hospitals. Our findings did not support this view. All but one of the wardens and staff in the present study had hospital backgrounds and training but had apparently managed to rid themselves of "institutional values" as measured by Apte's standards. Apte's concept of what constitutes permissive-restrictiveness is not the only one that may be considered, however. The most "permissive" hostel in our study, run by non-hospital-trained staff whose ideology emphasised individual autonomy and development exercised a constraint on residents' autonomy which can be seen as greater than any on the Apte scale – that is, the obligation to try to change as a person, through compulsory attendance at group meetings. Such a "treatment" approach must also to some extent conflict with the attempt to create a home-like atmosphere for residents.

Other small signs of conflicting aspects of hostel life were observed by the research team. For example, in many hostels the residents are called by their christian names but they do not call the warden by his or her christian name – though they sometimes use the christian names of other care staff. There may be notice boards in the hall, books for residents to sign in when they go out and when they come back in. Medicines may be put out in the front hall, where anyone can see them, or people may queue up to get them at the office door. These all seem to the visitor to suggest an "institutional" approach, although residents do not always resent them. Similarly, meals are served on the plate, so that people do not have the opportunity to help themselves to vegetables or second helpings. How much do such things matter?

Unlike the practices discussed earlier in this paper, they have no obvious positive value for the residents. They serve to emphasise the fact that residents' status is not yet that of the ordinary citizen, without increasing the "enabling" effect of the supportive environment. The hostel staff may not be aware of this. Residents themselves may not be aware of it either.

The relationship between wardens and residents must be difficult for both parties to work out. Apte (1968) discusses the contradictions inherent in the situation when wardens and their wives are, in theory, part of the "family environment" of the hostel but in practice withdraw when they can to their own living quarters and never share meals with the residents. Part of the problem is that "family" concepts usually encompass groups consisting of parents and children, not groups of adults organised on democratic principles.

Nevertheless, the family analogy can be used, as we have used it above, to provide a different, less negative way of looking at some of the controls exercised by staff over residents. The staff, particularly wardens, can be seen as "parents" and some residents themselves describe wardens in this way. By extension, the "social treatment" which the environment of hostels is intended to provide can be conceptualised in terms of child-rearing. People handicapped by mental illness are thought to be unable to accept full responsibility for every aspect of their lives, as in the case of young children. They are also thought to be capable of learning and of personality growth and development, as are children. Parents teach children, by example and by precept, to behave in socially acceptable ways – to be clean and tidy, to be punctual, to be pleasant to others, to have a sense of responsibility and to exercise self-control. During this process, parents provide a stable and loving relationship but they also apply sanctions to control behaviour. The parent exercises authority and is more powerful than the child and it may be at this point that the analogy between the warden-resident and parent-child relationship is weakest and becomes least useful. The warden is undoubtedly more powerful than the resident but the resident is not a child and should not be treated like one except in those ways we have described as "enabling" him to develop without diminishing his autonomy. The corollary to this, however, is that wardens should not have to feel as responsible for residents as parents feel for their children.

An important parental function is that of protection. Adult residents, to put it simply, must be allowed to be "at risk" in ways which are unacceptable for children. They must also have a greater degree of reciprocity with staff than is practicable between children and parents. Udall (1972), illustrating this point, quotes the warden showing him around a hostel who said, "This is Mildred's room – she likes her bits and pieces around her as you can see," and he comments, "one wonders how (the warden) would react if Mildred burst into his house with a similarly patronising remark." In this situation, it is possible to make the relationship between wardens residents one of equality –

69

the warden need not treat Mildred that way and it is arguable that parents need not treat their children that way either. When it comes to exercising authority to ask residents to leave, the situation is somewhat different. Then the status of resident may be that of an adult, even in this "power" relationship, since he will presumably have accepted, as an adult, the conditions on which he may continue to live in the hostel. Similar situations occur in student hostels and in ordinary agreements between landladies and lodgers.

Some of these problems may simply be inherent in the situation of staff and residents living together. If the positive aspects of supervision could be continued without wardens sharing accommodation with residents, different orders of relationship might develop. We have suggested above that the "caring" aspects of the so-called restrictive practices described by Apte may have positive value for residents, who benefit from having their medication regularly, from having someone who knows and cares whether they are at home or away. They benefit from contact with people experienced in recognizing and dealing with the specific problems of mental illness. The negative aspects of supervision by resident staff appear to lie in unnecessary extensions of "parental" responsibility. It is possible that paternalism could not have been avoided up to now because the populations of hostels have included many people who have lived in mental hospitals for very long periods and who have therefore suffered not only from their illness but also from some degree of institutionalism. The proposed policy of short-term in-patient care, if implemented, will mean that such populations will eventually disappear, and an important function of hostels will be to prevent the worst aspects of institutionalism while providing the positive aspects of care and support that we have described. The baby must not be thrown out with the bath water.

Creer and Wing (1974, 1975) have described a group of people with schizophrenia living at home who might well do much better in some kind of hostel environment, with maximum concern but minimum paternalism.

The "new" long-stay population described by Mann and Cree (1974) could probably live in similar accommodation, given suitable day-time care or occupation away from the hostel for those who cannot work. No doubt the amount and kind of supervision would need to be worked out for different groups of people and for individuals within groups, as is done now in many hostels where some residents take care of a weekly supply of their own drugs.

One model for such accommodation could be the type of scheme provided for the elderly, where each person has his own inviolable living space but willingly accepts the daily contact with the warden who lives separately but very nearby. Some communal living facilities, perhaps including one cooked meal a day, could be provided. In this kind of situation, some variation in personal standards for residents would have to be allowed. For example, the uniform neatness and orderliness which we have seen in most, though not all, hostels would very probably have to be sacrificed and this would be just one of the elements of risk that would be the inevitable concomitant of a reduction in paternalism.

The most encouraging finding in our pilot study was the high quality of the environments provided by the hostels seen. We can say with some certainty that the poverty of the environment previously found in some hospital wards did not exist on any of them. Residents were not subjected to routines which stripped them of their individuality. They came and went freely, with only the most minimal restraints. They were able to have personal possessions and to make personal relationships. The fact that, in spite of their reasonable living conditions, and their ability to work, many were still, to some degree, socially withdrawn, argues strongly that they may have reached a 'plateau' in their return to health and would be unable, whatever the circumstances, to advance further. They could, however, deteriorate in less favourable environments.

Provision of long-term care for some people may itself be thought of as long-term treatment, rather than failed rehabilitation. If there is no other way to maximise the potential and minimise the handicaps of those with long-lasting (i.e. chronic) mental illness, provision of social environments truly becomes treatment, albeit palliative rather than curative. The value of palliative treatments for any illness or condition can be defended both on humanitarian and economic grounds. If such a point of view is accepted, a more realistic approach to planning for the future could be made.

There would be no need, of course, to assume that *no one* would move out of sheltered accommodation, any more than it has been correct to assume in the past that everyone, once "rehabilitation" had taken place, *should* move out. Those who want to live in other ways should have every assistance and encouragement to do so. There were many people who could have left the hostels we saw if some of the practical impediments to their leaving had been removed. As we report elsewhere (Hewett, Ryan and Wing, op. cit.), the majority of the people in the pilot study were without significant family and social networks. They were some of the single homeless people who form a large group in London but with the added disadvantages which followed from their psychiatric history. They earned low incomes and were competing for accommodation in a situation of severe housing shortage. The standard of living they could buy for themselves on the open market was much lower than the one they had become accustomed to in the hostels, where their living expenses were subsidised by their supporting local authorities. The goal was set for most of them was to move out into a solitary bed-sitting room, where they would have to meet, without subsidy, unaccustomed responsibility for paying bills, for buying and preparing food, and for dealing without help with every minor crisis of daily living. They would have to remember and feel motivated to take their medication, to get up in time to go to work and to maintain, without prompting or encouragement, acceptable standards of appearance and behaviour. Such a goal may be unrealistic even for people who have achieved such a high level of recovery. Tidmarsh and Wood (1972) have shown that without support they may readily drift towards prisons, reception centres and destitution. A variety of residential environments in addition to hostels would be necessary to prevent such a drift.

The most familiar alternative is the group home. These can vary in kind as much as seems necessary for the residents. Some are conceived as small half-way houses from which residents are expected to move on. Others are intended from the outset to offer permanent homes. Not having resident professional staff, they can be entirely without support, having only a rent collector calling, or they can have varying degrees of support from social workers employed by voluntary bodies and from social service departments. Unpaid volunteers may take an interest in them. Support may be intensive in the early days of residence and gradually reduced over time. They have often been used to rehouse people who have known each other through living in mental hospitals for twenty years or more but there is no reason why they should not also be the next step for people ready to leave hostels. Mann and Cree (1976) report that both voluntary bodies and local authorities are currently making more use of group homes than of hostels. Setting them up involves lower capital outlay and avoids the problems of staffing that arise with hostels, including that of high running costs.

The papers by Olsen, Slater and Smith in this volume show that boarding out with landladies offers another alternative to hostel care and another stage in non-hospital care to which a resident may progress. These too have the advantage of being very flexible, with as many variations as there are landladies. They may provide much or little support, very limited or very varied social experience and choice of companionship. They are only practicable, however, where the local population includes a number of landladies who are willing to participate and who have suitable rooms available. This is not always the case in London boroughs and Mann and Cree (op. cit.) found that local authorities, throughout the country, with one notable exception, had experienced great difficulty in their attempts to set up such a service.

The pilot study showed clearly that the Apte measure of the environments offered by hostels was inadequate to discriminate between them regarding important elements of those environments. There has been a tendency to assume that supervised hostels with trained staff provide more intensive support than alternative forms of community care and to place them at one end of a continuum with ordinary landladies at the other. However, we found that staff/resident ratios varied widely from hostel to hostel, which could have seriously affected staff/resident contact. In some, where residents were in full-time work, staff/resident interaction was limited effectively to about three hours on working days and variable amounts at weekends. Living with an ordinary landlady might provide much more personal support and interaction than was possible in a hostel and a landlady might well provide as many of the "caring" aspects of supervision described above as hostel staff. If landladies were backed up by trained social workers it is arguable that "lodgers" would receive more intensive support than hostel residents. Measures to assess the nature and intensity of support in different environments will have to be devised in order to take their analysis a step further than Apte's approach allows. It is hoped that this will be possible in the next stage of this study.

Our evidence suggests that it would be useful to mount an experimental study in which some residents from the local authority hostel were provided with financially subsidised accommodation in group homes with social work support or a non-resident warden as in schemes for the elderly while a similar group, matched on clinical and social variables, stayed in the hostel. The progress of these groups could be monitored over a period of one year. The functions of the wardens or supervisors would need to be clearly defined. During this time, a third group of hospital patients similarly matched could be given the vacated hostel places and their progress similarly monitored. Until some of the hostel residents are given the opportunity to live in a less sheltered environment, we shall not know whether they are capable of doing so or not.

Summary

The results of replicating Apte's (1968) analysis of hostel environments have been discussed in detail. Although our pilot study yielded evidence on eight hostels only, these eight environments were sufficiently similar in terms of

Apte's measure of restrictive/permissive practices, to suggest that the measure must be modified, in order to increase discrimination between them and to describe the differing living environments which they offer adequately.

The small number of so-called "restrictive" practices still retained by a majority of hostels may in fact be necessary to enable residents to hold down jobs in open employment. If this is so, it suggests that some degree of long-term support will be necessary even for those who appear to be most able, as well as for the more handicapped. Our limited evidence also suggests that factors external to the hostels, such as low income and shortage of other accommodation, were more effective in preventing some residents leaving, than any factors within the environments of the hostels.

The relationship between hostel staff and hostel residents has been discussed and we have suggested that the quasi-parental role, particularly for wardens, may be helpful in some respects but may give rise to conflict and contradiction in others.

APPENDIX

Apte's study was carried out in several phases, each concerning different numbers both of people and hostels. In the first phase, data were collected on 851 men and women who were first admissions to 25 "transitional" hostels during a period of one year (1962-1963). These 25 hostels provided a total of 449 places. Postal questionnaires were completed by "senior administrators ultimately responsible for the operation of the hostels". Further data were obtained regarding 341 first admissions to 14 "non-transitional hostels", some of these being long-stay by intention, the remainder being so defined by Apte but not by original intention. Again, these data were collected from administrators by means of postal questionnaire. All this information covered a study period of one year, 1962-1963.

In 1963, data regarding staff in 25 transitional hostels were gathered, apparently again by postal questionnaire. In 1965, Apte appears to have visited the 25 transitional hostels in order to administer his Hospital/Hostel Practices Profile. At this time he also visited 17 hospital wards, from which residents had been referred to hostels, in order to administer the Profile in these wards and compare the environments they provided with those of the hostels.

At an unspecified time staff and administrators concerned with a sub-sample of 13 "transitional" hostels, all run by local authorities, were contacted and information on these 13 was obtained regarding administrative and rehabilitative aspects of hostel functioning. At yet another time, 1st March 1965, some data were gathered on 385 people currently resident in an unspecified number of "half-way houses".

Note 1
The four voluntary bodies were the Mental After Care Association, the Richmond Fellowship, the Cheshire Foundation, and the Jewish Welfare Board.

References

Apte, R. Z. (1968), *Half-way House,* Occasional Papers on Social Administration, No. 27. London: Bell.

Barton, R. (1959), *Institutional Neurosis,* 2nd edition. Bristol: Wright, 1966.

Clark, D. H. (1964), *Administrative Therapy.* London: Tavistock Publications.

Clark, D. H. and Cooper, L. W. (1960), "Psychiatric Half-way Hostel – A Cambridge Experiment". *The Lancet, 12 March 1960.* pp. 588-90.

Creer, C. (1975), "Living with Schizophrenia", *Social Work Today 6,* pp. 2-7.

Creer, C. and Wing, J. K. (1974), *"Schizophrenia at Home".* National Schizophrenia Fellowship, 29 Victoria Road, Surbiton, Surrey.

Durkin, E. (1971), *Hostels for the Mentally Disordered.* Young Fabian Pamphlet, No. 24. London.

Fletcher, J. C. (1970), *Mental Health Hostels: progress and problems.* Aylesbury: Buckinghamshire County Council.

Freudenberg, R. K. (1967), Theory and practice of rehabilitation of the psychiatrically disabled. *Psych. Quart., 41,* 698.

Gunzburg, H. C. (1973), The Physical Environment of the Mentally Handicapped. *Brit. J. Ment. Subnormality,* December 1973.

Hewett, S., Ryan, P. and Wing, J. K. (1975), "Living Without the Mental Hospitals". *J. Soc. Pol. 4,* 391-404.

Mann, S. and Cree, W. (1976), "'New' long-stay psychiatric patients: A national sample of 15 mental hospitals in England and Wales, 1972/3. *Psychol. Med. 6,* pp. 603-16.

Mountney, G. H. (1965), Local Authority Psychiatric Hostels. *Brit. J. Psychiat. Soc. Work 20.*

Mountney, G. H. (1968), Adjusting the Environment – Transitional Accommodation. In: *"Psychiatric Care in the Community".* Proc. Conference Roy. Soc. Health.

Raush, H. L. with Raush, C. L. (1968), *The Half-Way House Movement – A Search for Sanity.* New York: Appleton.

Ryan, P. and Hewett, S. H. (1976), A pilot study of hostels for the mentally ill, *Social Work Today, 6,* 25, 774-778.

Tidmarsh, D. and Wood, S. M. (1972), Psychiatric aspects of destitution. In: *Evaluating a Community Psychiatric Service.* Eds: Wing, J. K. and Hailey, A. M. London: Oxford University Press.

Udall, Tim (1972), Institution or Community? *Social Work Today,* 7 Sept. 1972.

Wing, J. K. and Brown, G. W. (1970), *Institution and Schizophrenia.* Cambridge University Press.

5: Patterns of Residential Care:

A Study of Hostels and Group Homes used by four Local Authorities to support Mentally Ill People in the Community

Peter Ryan and J. K. Wing

1. Introduction

In this chapter, we shall summarise the results of a survey of community accommodation for people who had previously been in psychiatric hospitals, undertaken in order to describe the characteristics and roles of residents and staff, to ascertain the place of the units within the overall pattern of services provided by health, social and voluntary agencies, and to estimate the cost of the units.

The administrative and financial climate in which the work was carried out is best summed up by a quotation from the Government White Paper on services for the mentally ill. 'Even in favourable circumstances it would obviously take a long term programme to achieve in all parts of the country the kind of change we are advocating . . . In present economic circumstances there is clearly little or no scope for substantial additional expenditure on health and personal social services, at least for the next few years . . . Without increased community resources the numbers in mental hospitals cannot be expected to fall at the rate they may otherwise have done. Delay in building up local services must mean that it is unlikely that we shall be able to see in every part of the country the kind of service we would ideally like within even a twenty-five year horizon.' (DHSS, 1975).

In spite of the pessimism of this approach, we thought it useful to investigate the extent to which currently available provision was meeting the needs of the 'adult mentally ill'* and whether recommendations could be

---

*The term 'adult mentally ill' is misleading in many ways. The people with whom we are concerned are not acutely ill, although most have been at some time in the past and some have residual symptoms. The term 'mentally handicapped' has come to be reserved for people with severe intellectual retardation, otherwise it would be very appropriate. We shall use the designation 'mentally disabled' to cover the various impairments found in people using these hostels and group homes.

made that would improve effectiveness without necessarily costing a great deal of money. The background of previous work has been discussed by Sheila Hewett in an earlier chapter. Even during the recent period of financial restriction, there has been a good deal of experiment with various forms of care. The group home has taken over from the hostel as the most rapidly developing type of provision. In addition, imaginative ways of using local resources have been found, resulting in closer co-operation with housing departments or housing associations, and a variety of additional types of accommodation such as supervised bed-sitters, boarding out schemes, and sheltered flats. Unfortunately, more often than not, they are not all available within an integrated network of local services. Gross regional discrepancies still exist. One area may have a hostel, but no group homes, and vice versa. In 1975, 24 out of 108 local authorities in England still provided no non-hospital accommodation at all for the mentally ill.

A further study was therefore designed, based on four local authority areas in which a range of accommodation was available and where innovations had been introduced that might have useful implications for planning services in other areas.

2. The Study Population

The term 'adult mentally ill' was defined to include anyone aged over 16 who had experienced psychiatric inpatient care. There was no upper age limit, but those with dementia, the mentally retarded, and people with special problems such as alcoholism and addiction were excluded. For the purpose of the study, three patterns of service provision were selected, each of which was innovative in certain respects. The first pattern comprised local authority hostels and group homes in Camden, Islington, Newham and Redbridge. The second comprised group homes set up by a voluntary association (Camden Association of Mental Health). The third comprised co-ordinated provision by a network of agencies including the local authority housing department (Redbridge), a psychiatric hospital with a community nursing department and occupational therapy preparation, (Goodmayes Hospital), and a voluntary body (Goodmayes Housing Association). Figure 1 summarises the four hostels and three networks of group homes investigated.

Three of the four hostels were intended to be short-stay while the fourth had a mixed function. Hostels therefore emphasized a rehabilitative approach while group home supervisors placed more emphasis on a maintaining and supporting role. Hostel 3 had two ancilliary units attached. One was a

78

Figure 1

Summary of accommodation investigated

Unit	Authority	Characteristics of accommodation provided
Hostel 1	Camden L.A.	Small, local authority short-stay rehabilitation hostel in converted house, whose staff were using a number of innovative rehabilitation techniques
Group Home Network 1	Camden L.A. and Camden A.M.H.	3 group homes sponsored by voluntary body, supervised in co-ordination with social service department
Hostel 2	Islington L.A.	20-bed purpose-built local authority short-stay hostel, where the staff were attempting to maximise resident participation by running the hostel on corporate management lines
Hostel 3	Newham L.A.	Large purpose-built local authority short *and* long-stay hostel, whose staff also provided supervision for a group home preparation unit, a self-care annexe, and a block of flats. Overall supervision was provided by a community psychologist
Hostel 4	Redbridge L.A.	Small local authority hostel in converted house
Network 2	Redbridge L.A., Goodmayes Hospital and Goodmayes Housing Association	Network of 3 group homes, independent flats and hotels, supervised by community nursing unit, administered by voluntary housing association, houses provided by housing department
Network 3	Redbridge L.A. and Claybury Hospital	Network of 5 group homes, supervised by social workers, houses provided by housing department

preparation unit on the first floor, designed for a group of residents who would later be transferred to a group home. The other was a self-care annexe; a purpose-built block of seven bed-sitters, each with its own kitchen, 50 yards down the road from the hostel.

The social services departments and hospitals involved readily co-operated by providing a list of people being supported financially in after-care accommodation for the mentally ill, and by giving permission for staff and clients to be interviewed. In all, 93 residents were interviewed; a further 29 either failed to turn up at interview appointments, or refused interview. Forty-five of the 93 people interviewed were living in local authority hostels, 39 were living in eleven different group homes, and nine were resident in two supervised hotels.

3. Methods of Description

Six techniques of data collection were used:—

(i) Interview with Residents, in order to ascertain age, sex, marital status, employment history, length of hospitalisation, social contact with family and friends, attitude to leaving, etc. Many items could be checked from records. (Results are summarised in section 4.1 and Appendix 1).

(ii) The MRC Social Performance Schedule was adapted from a behaviour scale that had been extensively tested in hospital settings (Wing and Brown, 1970). The schedule covers psychiatric symptoms, dependency, self-care, help with chores, contribution to group meetings, and residents' attitudes. It was completed after discussing each resident with members of staff. (Results are summarised in section 4.2 and Appendix 2).

(iii) The Moos Perceived Environment Scale is a 60-item questionnaire (Moos, 1974), adapted for use in British hostels and group homes. Each of the items defines an aspect of the social environment, in terms of personal relationships, treatment, and organisation. Each also functions as an open-ended question, allowing the respondents to give an account of the social environment in which they lived or worked. The scales were only administered to residents. (Results are summarised in section 4.3 and Appendix 3).

(iv) The Decision-making Schedule was used to assess the amount of resident participation perceived by staff and residents as occurring in their particular environment. The scale sets out a total of 23 situations that are likely to occur in any community setting for the mentally ill. Each resident and staff member living or working in a particular setting was then asked who would decide

what would happen with respect to each of the 23 situations. Three options were given. First, that the residents would decide (i.e. a situation of maximum independence); secondly, that a process of consultation existed with both staff and residents jointly participating in the decision; thirdly, that staff alone decided, without involving residents in any way in the decision. (Results are summarised in section 4.4 and Appendix 4.)

(v) The Rehabilitation Index was completed in conjunction with the social performance schedule. Each staff member interviewed was asked whether the behaviour rated on the social performance scale was an indication that the resident was well or poorly adjusted with respect to this particular element of his behaviour. If an indication of poor adjustment was given, the staff member was asked what either he or another staff member was doing to facilitate better adjustment. This kind of assessment was derived for every resident in each of the four hostels. (Results are summarised in section 4.5 and Appendix 5). The situation in the group homes was quite different and the index was not used there.

(vi) Interview with Staff, in order to obtain information about their work experience, qualifications, job satisfaction, and training needs. (See Section 4.6, and also Appendix 6 for analysis of amount of staff time available per resident).

4. Comparisons between Hostels and Group Homes

4.1 Characteristics of residents

There were marked differences between the groups of people living in hostels and group homes, summarised in Appendix 1. In general, the indices suggested that those living in group homes had been and were more disadvantaged and more handicapped. Group home residents were older (only 10% under 45), had spent a longer period in hospital (71% more than five years) and a longer period in the home (53% more than two years), were less likely to have had a sexual relationship (only 57%, even when functioning at their best, and only 11% at the time of the survey), and were less likely to be employed (62% were not even attending a day centre). Among those whose diagnosis at the time of the last hospital admission was known, 76% had been regarded as schizophrenic and 15% as having an affective psychosis (mania or severe depression). Three-quarters had no desire to leave the group home. Another characteristic was that two-thirds of the group home residents were women.

There was little difference between the two groups on marital state; more

81

than 70% of each had never married. However, it should be recalled that the hostel group were younger. Another point of similarity was the low income level; very few residents in either group had more than £10 per week.

By contrast with those in group homes, residents of hostels were more likely to be men, to be younger (70% under 45), had had less hospital experience (though more than a third had been in hospital for a total of more than five years) and a shorter stay in the hostel (two-thirds less than a year), were more likely to have had a sexual relationship when functioning at their best (82%, although only 25% currently), and were more likely to be in open employment or some other form of occupation (55%). Schizophrenia was the commonest diagnosis (43%), but neurosis (28%) and 'personality disorder' (19%) were also common. A sizeable minority (41%) wanted to leave the hostel but the majority wanted to stay.

These differences suggest different types of selective process into hostels and group homes. The latter accepted more 'old long-stay' patients, with a history of prolonged handicap and an apparently smaller chance of eventually achieving independence. Hostels, on the other hand, also accepted younger people with less handicapping conditions and a possibly better prognosis. The former group might be expected to be more amenable but more withdrawn; the latter more troublesome but more lively. If so, such differences should be borne in mind when considering differences between the respective social environments.

4.2 Social performance

There was very little difference between hostel and group home residents on items specifically designed to describe socially withdrawn behaviour, such as participation in group meetings, or active approaches to staff. The fact that staff spent less time in the group homes may have led to an under-rating of withdrawal there. However, it was the commonest 'problem' recognised by staff in both settings, as will be decribed in section 4.5. Nearly a third of the hostel members named four or more 'friends' among the other residents, compared with only 19% group home members, probably because hostels contained more people than homes.

The amount of contact with the local community was limited in both groups; fewer than 20% had visited a friend or relative during the previous week, and 23% had no such contact for at least six months. Eighty-four per cent had gone out by themselves during the previous week but only 38% had done so in the company of a fellow resident.

The main differences between the two groups were related to disturbed behaviour. The details are given in Appendix 2. Hostel residents were more demanding, more unstable, had poorer manners, and showed more bizarre behaviour or speech. This is consistent with their being younger, having had a breakdown more recently, and being more likely to have had a diagnosis of 'personality disorder'.

Two ratings made by staff indicated the expected greater degree of disability among group home residents. One is a rating of overall degree of handicap (48% had a severe and lasting impairment compared with 13% in hostels); the other was a rating of the likelihood of successful resettlement (74% were thought to need permanent shelter compared with 19% in hostels).

4.3 Social environments

The differences between the social environments, as measured by residents' perceptions rated on the Moos Scales, are summarised in Appendix 3. There were significant differences between hostels and group homes on only four scales: Autonomy; Practical orientation; Anger and hostility; Staff control.

'Autonomy' is a measure of how far residents feel encouraged (or allowed) to be self-sufficient in their personal affairs. Group home residents had much greater freedom according to this index (88% in the highest category, compared with 33% of hostel residents).

'Practical orientation' is a measure of the extent to which the residents' environment is orientated towards preparing them for independent living by encouraging them to cook, clean and shop for themselves. Group home residents had more responsibility according to this index (25% in the highest category, compared with 7% of hostel residents).

'Freedom to express anger' is a measure of the extent to which a resident feels encouraged (or allowed) to express anger to other residents and staff. Hostel residents reported more such freedom. (Group home residents were, in any case, rarely reported by staff as showing anger or hostility).

'Staff control' is a measure of the extent to which staff retain control of residents by laying down sanctions on unwanted behaviour. Hostel staff appeared more controlling according to this index. (The same trend appears, though not significantly in ratings of the scale representing 'order and organisation'.)

These results are compatible with those presented in sections 4.1 and 4.2, in that they suggest an attempt to deal with the more disturbed behaviour of hostel residents, while group home residents are left to their own devices to a much greater extent. Since each of the items in the Moos scale was presented, not only as a fixed choice between two alternative answers ('Yes' and 'No') but as an open-ended question, to which the residents' answers were recorded, it is possible to illuminate the statistical differences with examples of comments. These comments are considered in more detail elsewhere (Ryan, 1979) but a few are given here by way of illustration.

Group home tenants often commented on the experience of leading a relatively independent life: 'We all go our different ways; we please ourselves'; 'Before I came, the others neglected it, the grass in the garden was knee-high. I've got rid of five trees myself. I sawed them down and dug them up'; 'Before, you were in an institution. Here you are comfortable, you can do just as you like'. Sometimes, however, a resident felt in need of more staff support than was available: 'I would like him [the visiting social worker] to listen to what I have to say . . . but I don't think I would be inclined to ask him for help. I would feel he was not bothered to listen to me'.

Comments in the hostels were more concerned with tension and hostility and staff supervision: 'When there is a big disagreement amongst residents, staff will encourage discussion, but a lot of disagreement is hidden, so staff don't hear of it. It gets buried until something triggers it off'; 'There is a lot of mischief – vendettas even'; 'They talk about their problems all the time, you can't get away from it'; 'You feel like you're being watched somehow – it makes it kind of official'.

4.4. Participation

The data collected from residents on the basis of the Moos scales could be checked from the decision-making scales, the results of which are presented in Appendix 4. Considering, first, all the types of decisions included in the scale (Table 4.1), it is clear that there is a good deal of variability between settings but, overall, residents of group homes report that just over half are taken by them on their own responsibility, compared with just over one third of hostel residents. Hostel 3 has a preparation unit and a self-care annexe which naturally place more emphasis on responsibility in residents, but if these two units are omitted the lack of decision-making by Hostel 3 residents becomes very pronounced. It is also particularly evident in Hostel 4. Hostels 1 and 2 place relatively more emphasis on joint consultation but do not give much autonomy to residents. Among the three group home networks, No. 2 places relatively more emphasis on staff decision-making.

In the case of 'management' decisions (Table 4.2), there is more overall emphasis on staff responsibility, as would be expected, but a marked tendency for more responsibility to be taken in group homes is evident.

The differences between hostels 1 and 2, where relatively more decisions were taken following joint consultation, and hostels 3 and 4, where most were taken by staff, cannot be accounted for in terms of numbers of residents, staff-resident ratio, staff training, or size of the premises. All four hostels were managed by local authority Social Service Departments. Further interpretation of these results will be withheld until data from the rehabilitaion index and the staff interviews have been presented.

4.5 Rehabilitation index

The rehabilitation index has two components. First, the staff member is asked whether any of the items rated in the Social Performance Schedule (see section 4.2) are currently seen as problems that require staff intervention. Second, each item seen as needing intervention is discussed with staff in order to discover what action is being taken. The results given here are based on a content analysis of the replies. Since staff contacts with residents of group homes are very sparse (see section 4.6) the following data are related only to hostels.

Staff in the four hostels gave very similar lists of behaviour regarded as problematical. A list showing the rank orders is given in Appendix 5 (Table 5.1). The commonest single problem (16% of all the items mentioned) was avoidance of social contact. Several other problem behaviours (poor performance of chores, 13%; overdependence, 10%; underinvolvement, 7%; and underassertion, 5%) were possibly part of the same syndrome. Other problem behaviours mentioned were overassertion, 11%; work difficulties, 7%; anxiety about leaving, 7%; inconsistency, 6%; low self-esteem, 6%; depression, 5%; and inappropriate social behaviour, 5%.

Each hostel resident was seen as presenting, on average, 5.9 problems, and each staff member had a 'case-load' of 18.1 problems. The content of staff statements about these problems is analysed elsewhere (Ryan, 1979) and only two examples are given here. One resident in Hostel 1 (withdrawn and underinvolved) was described as follows: 'She tends not to make contact with us unless something's very wrong. I'm frustrated in that I know she feels better when she does talk, yet you really have to dig it out of her. Often she won't talk unless she's bursting. All I can do is to let her know I'm always available.'

85

A resident in Hostel 2 was overassertive: 'You have to respond to her whether you want to or not. She interferes into everything and is very accusing. You just try to resist her attempts at annoying you and point out what she is doing and that you are not interested in playing her games. You have to do this without rejecting her. This is very difficult. You also have to encourage her to take her medication which she tends not to do when she's high.'

These two statements illustrate not only the problem behaviour also the way staff tried to cope with it. In analysing these responses, a distinction was drawn between technical and non-technical skills. Interpersonal, social and community skills were included under the heading of 'technical'. By 'interpersonal' skill was meant techniques applicable by the staff member in a dyadic situation, with the aim of alleviating the mental and emotional stress of the resident, and of increasing his capacity to cope effectively with his environment. This would include behaviour modification techniques, contract bargaining, family therapy and insight counselling. By using his 'social' skills the staff member would hope to achieve the same aims by means of manipulating the social milieu of the residents. Examples of 'social' skills would be allowing the resident to participate in selecting new residents, extending or shortening the length of stay, or establishing regular house meetings. 'Community' skills could be used, again for the same ends, to liaise with an area social worker, a local volunteer, or the Housing Department, so as to make a group home available. Such skills, it was assumed, would require a degree of professional training. 'Non-technical' skills, on the other hand, could be acquired through everyday experience, without specialist training e.g. common-sense advice, encouragement to participate socially, engaging in conversation, prompting and reminding, joining in leisure activities, and specific tuition. A nil entry was made if no intervention was specified when a problem was identified by a member of staff.

Table 5.2 in Appendix 5 summarises the types of intervention made in the hostels. In all four (but particularly in Hostels 3 and 4) no intervention at all was made in a substantial proportion of problems; 24% overall. This was particularly true of the commonest problem, avoidance of social contact, which attracted no intervention in 41% of cases where it was mentioned. Non-technical interventions were common (52% overall) and there was very little difference between hostels. The most frequently used techniques were encouragement and support (17%), and advice (6%). Technical skills were used to deal with only 25% of problems overall, but more commonly (33%) in Hostels 1 and 2. The most frequent technical skills used were monitoring and feedback (8%) and insight counselling (5%). Hostel 1 staff, particularly, had tried to establish a 'therapeutic' milieu and used techniques such as contract bargaining, desensitisation, family therapy and sensitivity groups. There was a weekly budget planning group and a weekly staff-resident meeting. Use was also made of community volunteers. Nevertheless, even in this hostel, half the interventions reported by the staff in response to problem behaviour were non-technical, and in a further 17% of instances no intervention was made at all.

A general feature of all four hostels was the relative neglect of socially withdrawn residents, although this was the commonest problem reported by staff. Because of their smaller size and greater staffing ratio, it is usually assumed that hostels should be able to devote more attention to this problem than hospitals. We are unable to report comparative data but it appears that social withdrawal remains a problem that hostel staff find very difficult to counter.

4.6 Staff roles

(i) Time available

The staff time available to residents in hostels and group homes is shown in Appendix 6. All the hostel staff were attached full-time to one unit and had no other responsibilities. All the group home staff had other duties and tended to fit in their supervisory responsibilities as a relatively small part of their overall task. This accounts for the fact that far more staff time is available to hostel residents (11.9 hours per resident per week) than to group home residents (0.1 hour per resident per week). The staff time for hostel residents (e.g. 24 hours per resident per week in Hostel 1) does not, of course, mean that each individual received this amount of attention; simply that this time was available. The differences between group home networks are accounted for by frequency of visiting. Each of the three group homes in Network 1, for example, was visited by its own social worker and volunteer (six different people in all). The social workers (one hospital-based, two from the local area teams) visited once a fortnight; the volunteers once a week. Network 2 homes were visited twice a week by members of the community nursing unit (hospital-based); each time for 20-40 minutes. Three of the group homes of Network 3 were visited weekly by a social worker, one group home was visited every two or three weeks, and one every four to six weeks.

(ii) Hostel staff

Eighteen hostel staff were interviewed. Their average was 30 years (range 23-

47). The mean time worked in their current post was 16 months. Twelve were single, four married and two divorced. Two had left school after completing 'O' or 'A' levels and had no further qualifications, seven had attended technical or teaching colleges, six had a university degree, and three had further professional qualifications.

Only three had a qualification in social work. Another was engaged in in-service training, one in a psychotherapy course, and three in a three-year evening course in group dynamics. Virtually all expressed a desire for further training, particularly in group dynamics, individual and family therapy, theories of personality development, and practical issues such as legislation and social security benefits.

There was much general satisfaction at the flexibility and informality of the work, the feeling that it called on the inner resources of staff, the support obtained from working in small communities, and the assumption that the work was socially valuable. Typical comments were: 'We're very lucky here; everyone can put their own ideas forward about hostel policy, with a sporting chance of getting them accepted . . . It's the first job I've had where I've been able to try things out'; 'It challenges me to exercise all my abilities'; 'Sometimes magical things happen, like a sudden unexpected act of spontaneity from someone you didn't think was capable of it'. However, these advantages entailed corresponding frustrations; 'Bureaucracies aren't geared to self-help, since it involves putting people at risk, which frightens management'; 'I feel I'm not seen as a person [by the residents] but as a staff member'; 'I spend too many hours in this one building, particularly in the evenings and at weekends'; 'I get depressed at times. I wonder if anything is really happening'; 'It's difficult to know whether you're doing any good – whether you've got a right to interfere in their lives'.

All the hostel staff interviewed thought that contact with supervisors was at least adequate. Seven, however, thought that communication with managers was poor: 'He doesn't know anything about the work and doesn't understand'; 'We get feedback of disapproval but not of approval'. There were many comments on administrative delays, for example over repairs or maintenance. Sometimes, management policy appeared unduly rigid as when a domestic cleaner had to be employed to do work that staff thought should be the responsibility of residents.

Hostel residents were chosen by community personnel, primarily by hostel staff themselves, but always after a probationary period, so that other residents had a considerable say in selection. This resulted in the exclusion of many severely impaired or disturbed individuals. At the time of the survey all hostels were underoccupied, one being only 60% full.

(iii) Group Home staff

Eight group home supervisors were interviewed. On average, they had been in post for 26 months. The average age was 29; four were married and four single. Six had been to university and two had attended technical colleges. Four had diplomas in social work, one was a state-registered nurse, and three were unqualified. Six of the eight thought additional part-time or day release training might be useful.

All felt their work was socially valuable but most had reservations about the amount of support available to residents. At two of the three networks there were regular meetings with supervisors concerning the residents but in the third there was nothing of this kind. An unqualified worker in such circumstances could feel very isolated: 'Nobody in the office knows what you're doing, so there's no pool of experience to learn from. I tend to feel out on a limb without any idea of how the set-up as a whole is working'. Volunteers also had little supervision.

The uncertainty about aims led to similar comments to those made by hostel workers, perhaps rather more intense because of the lack of the cohesion found among groups of hostel staff: 'If I don't come they get upset, but if I do, nothing seems to happen'; 'Alice was manic and very difficult to live with. The other residents wanted to get rid of her back to hospital. I found it difficult to know how much I should persuade them to keep her'. The infrequent visits did not allow staff to keep much control of such situations. One social worker commented: 'It's hard to differentiate my role from the volunteer. I've asked the group if they want me to continue to come.' Similarly, residents had to be left very much to their own devices. They did not seem to gain very much from being with each other and the visiting staff member was not present often enough to influence the situation. 'For most of them, taking responsibility for themselves is as much as they can manage. They don't have any energy left over to help each other.'

Most supervisors called during the day rather than in the evenings. This meant that the 26% of tenants who were employed had very little contact with the supervisor. Many of the group homes had developed an arrangement whereby all the unemployed tenants would gather when the supervisor called. Thus the natural setting for supervision was the group context. Nonetheless, all the supervisors emphasised that they tried to ensure that any resident who wanted to see them individually could do so: 'Even though they're always together, quite often one will go into the kitchen to make tea, or another will doze off, so you do have the chance to talk to individual residents'.

All the supervisors emphasised that a key part of their job was to maximise the independence of their residents. 'I have to remember that it's their home, and when I go in, I'm there as their guest.' Quite often, this entailed resisting attempts by residents to pass over responsibility to staff. One supervisor, for example, was having a difficult time in persuading residents that they should choose what new cooker they should have; the residents would have been content for staff to decide.

Another important element in the staff role was monitoring the effectiveness with which residents dealt with the practical tasks involved in living independently in the community. If all was going well, it was simply necessary to praise and encourage the residents in their successful efforts at coping; if, however, either a particular resident, or the group as a whole, was coping inadequately with a task, then it would be the responsibility of the supervisor to intervene. Problems requiring intervention might be: interpersonal difficulties between two or more residents, self-neglect in clothing and personal appearance, social isolation, failure to budget adequately, or to cook or clean the house to a minimal standard, failure to pay the rent, or to take medication consistently.

Practically all group home tenants were referred from hospital. This meant that hospital doctors, nurses and social workers played the principal role in selection. The preparation unit in Goodmayes Hospital was a very useful means of discovering which residents would be most suitable.

5. Costs of Hostels and Group Homes (1975-6)

The framework chosen for cost comparison was that used by the Chartered Institute of Public Finance and Accountancy in their annual review of Local Authority Health and Social Service statistics. The same framework was used by the Finance Departments of each of the four boroughs in the survey. In addition, two cost ratios were computed for each hostel and for group home Network 2 ((see Appendix 7). The wage-net cost ratio defines the proportion of cost per resident week accounted for by payment of staff salaries. The income-cost ratio defines what proportion of total expenditure is met by income (primarily, but not entirely, income from residents).

So far as the hostels are concerned, costs per resident week varied between £41.96p (Hostel 3) and £61.21p (Hostel 2). The greatest single factor contributing to cost was staff salary, varying from 51% (Hostel 3) to 82%

90

(Hostel 4). Although resident rent covered only between 12.2% (Hostel 2) and 19.9% (Hostel 3) of total expenditure, leaving a local authority subsidy requirement of between 80.1% (Hostel 3) and 87.8% (Hostel 2), rents were none the less quite high. Since only a quarter of hostel residents were working, this meant in effect that centrally funded supplementary benefit was giving a 'hidden' local authority subsidy with respect to all unemployed residents.

Unlike the hostels, group home Network 2 was very nearly self-supporting in terms of running costs (£1.11p per resident week). Staff salary cost per resident week was £1.08p, as compared to £50.17p for hostel 4 (1975-76). There appear to be two main reasons for the large difference in salary cost between Network 2 and any of the hostels. First, only one staff member had responsibility for supervision of the group homes, whereas a full-time care-staff of three to six was normally employed in the hostels. Secondly, the amount of time spent per staff member was vastly less in Network 2 – an estimated three hours per week in each group home (nine hours in total). This contrasts with two hundred hours per week in a hostel with five fulltime staff members.

Rent (£4 per week) in Network 2 was much lower than in any of the hostels (35% of the rent charged in hostel 4). Nevertheless, income per resident week accounted for 81.3% of total expenditure in 1975-76, resulting in a cost per resident week of £1.11p. It should be noted, however, that food and laundry costs were not covered in the rental charge, so far as the group homes were concerned, whereas they were for the hostels.

6. Discussion

The residents of the group homes and hostels included in this survey were drawn from overlapping but generally different populations. Those from group homes were representatives of what has been called the 'old' long-stay hospital population; one third of them had spent over twenty years in hospital. Three-quarters had been given a diagnosis of schizophrenia. They were middle-aged to elderly, predominantly female, socially isolated, and unoccupied. Over half had been resident in the home for more than two years and three-quarters wanted to stay. They were withdrawn but not seriously demanding, unstable or bizarre in behaviour. Staff thought that three-quarters had a lasting impairment and would probably need sheltered accommodation permanently.

Residents of hostels, on the other hand, were more representative of people discharged from hospital after recent admissions. They were younger (60%

under 45), more likely to be men, with a shorter (though still substantial) history of hospitalisation. The diagnosis was much less likely to have been schizophrenia and they more often had a history of competent social relationships. However, at the time of the survey, they were as socially isolated as the residents of group homes, were rated as being as withdrawn and as giving rise to more problems because of demanding, unstable or bizarre behaviour. They were much more eager to leave the hostels. Staff regarded only 13% as having severe and lasting impairments and only 19% as being in need of permanent sheltered accommodation.

According to the Moos scales (as rated by residents), the group homes were high on autonomy and practical orientation, while the hostels were high on staff control but encouraged the expression of anger as a therapeutic technique. Decisions of all kinds were thought by residents of group homes to be more in their hands compared with hostel residents. These differences were presumably dictated by the more active rehabilitation approach in the hostels, made possible by the higher staff ratio, and reflecting a greater optimism about prognosis. Group homes, on the other hand were regarded as domestic environments where residents could settle permanently if they wished and where relatively little staff involvement was necessary. Both types of practice are, of course, represented in many hospitals, where there are 'hostels' with a rehabilitative orientation, and unstaffed villas for permanent residents. The environments we studied, however, were in ordinary residential streets and thus part of the community in a real sense, even though there was very little actual contact between residents and local people, apart from the volunteers.

The cheapness of group homes compared with hostels is strikingly apparent and raises a question as to how far some hostel residents could have gone directly to group homes. It is clear that, even in Hostel 1, only a third of the interventions made in response to problems reported by the staff were 'technical', in the sense that it would usually be regarded as necessary to have special training in order to carry them out. (We were not, of course, in a position to evaluate the effectiveness of the techniques used). Overall in the four hostels, only one quarter of the interventions were 'technical', half required no specialist training, and one quarter of the problems reported did not all attract any intervention at all. A lack of intervention was particularly evident in respect of behaviours such as social withdrawal, poor performance, overdependence and under-involvement, which accounted for nearly half of all those reported by staff. On the other hand, it might be argued that the social environment of the group homes is not sufficiently rich, given the potential for improvement demonstrated among the old long-stay hospital population (Wing and Brown, 1970).

One sub-group of emotionally unstable residents is particularly demanding of staff time in hostels and it would be inappropriate for them to move to less supervised settings. It would seem rational, however, to experiment both with a wider use of group homes for some hostel residents and with a greater degree of help (e.g. from occupational therapists) for the present group home residents.

Hostel 3 does, in fact, have a group home preparation unit and has set up three group homes, all the residents of which came from the hostel. Supervision needed to be fairly close to start with but could eventually reach a level of about one visit a week. The possibility of setting up some group homes where there is a higher level of supervision also requires consideration and experiment. Alternatively, more residents could be encouraged to attend day centres where supervision and occupational therapy was available (only 3% in our survey were doing so).

All the houses for the group homes in Networks 2 and 3 were provided by one housing department, a representative from which attended fortnightly rehabilitation committee meetings. Representatives of the community psychiatric nursing service and of the hospital occupational therapy staff also attended, as did a senior member of the Social Services Department. This regular meeting facilitated communication between all the agencies involved and also ensured that a house, supplied by the housing department, would be available for occupation at the time that the prospective group home tenants were ready to move in. The model has a great deal to commend it.

This survey did not include representatives of the 'new' long-stay group now accumulating in psychiatric hospitals (Mann and Sproule, 1972; Mann and Cree, 1975). Neither the hostels as at present constituted and still less the group homes, would be able (or willing) to deal with these more handicapped or disturbed people. It has been suggested that 'hospital hostels', with an appropriately domestic environment, might be a feasible solution (Wing, 1974) and the White Paper accepted this view (DHSS, 1975). The first such hostel has been set up at the Maudsley Hospital and is being evaluated. Hostels, of this kind, staffed by community nurses, could also be set up away from hospital sites, so long as there were adequate grounds. However, what is required in staff, in our view, is not so much a high level of professional training (since this can be provided by a supervisor) as an adequate experience of dealing with withdrawn and sometimes disturbed people and of how to provide a socially rich environment without at the same time expecting too much and precipitating further breakdown. The settings considered in this survey were not, of course, isolated, but parts of more or less comprehensive systems of medical and social care, each with its strengths and disadvantages. Several recent studies by the MRC Social Psychiatry Unit are highly relevant to the problem of how to organise and manage a comprehensive scheme of rehabilitation and long-term shelter for the 'adult mentally ill'. These include surveys of the 'new long-stay' population of psychiatric hospitals (Mann and Cree, 1975; Mann and Sproule, 1972), a current study of a 'hospital-hostel' for the new long-stay, an earlier survey of residential accommodation in three London boroughs (Hewett, Ryan and Wing, 1975; Ryan and Hewett, 1976), a study of hostels for destitute men (Leach and Wing, 1979a; Wing and Leach, 1979), and work with the families of people with schizophrenia (Creer, 1975; Creer and Wing, 1974; Vaughn and Leff, 1976; Wing, 1977). We have drawn on this experience in the suggestions that follow. Underlying them is the conviction that better services do not only require more staff and other resources but that better organisation and utilisation of existing resources, on the basis of knowledge that already exists, will often enable mentally disabled people to live more active and independent lives.

The underlying principle is that all mentally disabled individuals living in a defined geographical area should be regularly assessed in order to consider whether their current residential setting is the most appropriate one for them. This would include all those living in psychiatric hospitals, in various types of hostels and group homes, in bedsitters or supervised lodgings or with their own families. (Those attending day hospitals or centres would thus automatically be included as well). This raises formidable organisational and management problems since the agencies involved include hospitals, social service departments, housing authorities, employment offices, and a range of voluntary bodies. Each agency can undertake some form of assessment, though many do not; it is the implementation of decisions regarding movement between units that makes difficulties. Not only is each agency likely to undertake its own idiosyncratic form of assessment (very often in ignorance of factors familiar to other agencies, so that decisions made by one group will not be accepted by the others) but, because there is no co-ordinating mechanism, even decisions potentially acceptable to all may not be put into effect.

The first problem, therefore, is to set up co-ordinating machinery in each area. It is important that there should be no gaps in coverage even when health areas are not co-terminus with boroughs or counties. Everyone resident in psychiatric hospitals should be eligible for assessment and allocation to appropriate housing. Local social service departments have a statutory duty to provide for people 'ordinarily resident' in their areas but their duty towards others is discretionary. Similarly, housing departments and voluntary housing associations have discretion in how they allocate housing. The Housing (Homeless Persons) Act of 1977 enjoins housing departments to take responsibility for those who are otherwise homeless but this may well be interpreted as covering mainly 'local' homeless families, while those in hospital (or in accommodation for the destitute) who do not 'belong' to an area are 'homeless single persons'. If so, the gap must somehow be closed, otherwise the hospitals and the statutory and voluntary services for the destitute will be the only resources available, and they cannot provide sufficient accommodation of the requisite quality (Leach and Wing, 1979b).

We consider that people who stay as long as six months in a residential setting such as a hospital or hostel or centre, even if they do not 'belong' to the local area, should be regarded as eligible for local housing. As Tidmarsh, Wood and Wing (1972) pointed out, this entails special arrangements for funding, particularly in the case of areas where there is a high proportion of such people. Like them, we believe that this is a central government responsibility. It can never be solved on the basis of some fictitious 'parish of origin'.

The largest proportion of the mentally disabled do, in fact, 'belong' to an area and responsibility for providing residential accommodation is not in question. The problem is one of identification, assessment, co-ordination and implementation. We suggest that a Rehabilitation and Resettlement Committee should be set up in each area, attended by representatives of all the interested agencies (hospitals, social service, housing, employment, voluntary bodies), to set standards under these four headings and to monitor progress. The committee would need an input of information about occupancy and turnover from all the agencies represented. We suggested that a member of the staff of the local Social Services department could best undertake the role of liaison officer. The primary task of the committee would be to match the people needing accommodation (wherever they happened to be living at the time) to the facilities available and to put forward bids for new services as necessary.

For such a committee, and its liaison officer, to function most effectively it would be necessary for each agency to adopt a regular review system which had sufficient elements in common to ensure that decisions about movement between agencies could be made rationally. Both occupation and accommodation needs should be considered. We would suggest that all those who have spent as long as six months in care, whether in hospitals, hostels, homes, bedsitters, supervised lodgings, or day care, and some of the mentally disabled who are living with relatives but are known to be 'at risk' (e.g. where the relative is an elderly widow), should be reviewed in this way and at regular intervals thereafter. Any recommendations for a change in status that could not be implemented by the agency concerned would be put to the liaison officer.

The liaison officer would also become familiar with the specific features of each agency and receive returns of occupancy. In this way, over time, the committee would gain a picture of the needs of the area that would provide a rational basis for planning new services or for modifying existing ones. We would think that, under these circumstances, it would rarely be necessary to commission more purpose-built hostels but that adaptation of existing houses would usually be found more desirable because they were cheaper, less conspicuous, and provided a more domestic setting. The study by Seelye (1976) comes to the same conclusions.

One of the major findings of our survey is that half of the problem posed by residents' behaviour that were cited by hostel staff were associated with social withdrawal and underinvolvement. A similar result has been found in studies of hospitals and other types of hostel and there is little doubt that tenants of group homes were also very withdrawn. When hostel staff were asked to specify what response they had made to such problems, it transpired that in two-fifths of cases there had been no intervention at all. Even taking all types of problem into consideration, it appeared that interventions requiring technical skill were made only in about a quarter of cases, and presumably not all of these were effective. We think that there is a need for evaluation of various techniques of rehabilitation used in residential settings of all kinds in order to determine their longer-term effects and to provide a basis for staff training. Since so many of the residents of hostels and group homes had no employment and did not attend a day centre, attention should be paid to means of engaging their interest. One method would be to involve residents much more in the running of the house. This would mean helping not only with day-to-day 'domestic' problems but with management decisions. It is, of course, recognised that residents might adopt an unduly conservative admissions policy (wishing to exclude those who appeared too disabled or disturbed even though there was considerable potential for improvement) but influencing such attitudes is a matter for health education.

Many more residents could attend day centres or rehabilitation centres and it may be that much of the staff expertise should be concentrated in such settings. However, many residents, particularly in group homes, do not make use of the opportunities they are offered and there is insufficient staff time available to supervise attendance. The use of 'domiciliary' occupational therapists should be encouraged in order to foster an active programme within the homes.

In these ways, the residential and day care facilities in an area could, in time, become organised into a mental health service for the disabled, with the aim of raising overall standards toward the level of excellence which undoubtedly exists here and there at the moment.

Acknowledgements
This study could not have been undertaken without the co-operation of staff at Goodmayes and Claybury Hospitals, and at the Social Service and Finance departments of Camden, Islington, Newham and Redbridge, the Camden Association of Mental Health, and the Goodmayes Housing Association. Warmest thanks are due to the residents and staff of the hostels, group homes and hotels, all of whom welcomed the study, and not only gave the co-operation necessary for its completion, but also generous hospitality and interest in the project. The work was funded by the Department of Health and Social Security.

APPENDIX 1

Characteristics of Residents in Hostels and Group Homes

		Hostels (N45)	Group Homes (N39)
1.1	**Age**	%	%
	18–29	29	5
	30–44	41	5
	45–64	30	68
	65+	0	22
1.2	**Sex**		
	Male	63	32
	Female	37	68
1.3	**Marital Status**		
	Never married	71	76
	Married	4	0
	Divorced	25	16
	Widowed	0	8
1.4	**No lasting sexual relationship**		
	At present	75	89
	When functioning at best	18	43
1.5	**Present employment**		
	None	45	62
	Day centre	23	3
	Other (e.g. hospital O.T)	0	11
	Hospital training course	6	3
	Part-time open	12	11
	Full-time open	14	10

		Hostels (N45)	Group Homes (N39)
1.6	**Present cash income per week**	%	%
	Less than £5	0	27
	Less than £10	85	50
	Less than £15	12	23
	£16+	3	0

	1.7 **Total length of stay in hospital**		
	Less than 1 year	28	15
	Less than 5 years	36	14
	Less than 10 years	22	8
	Less than 20 years	10	30
	20+ years	4	33

1.8	**Diagnosis at last hospitalisation***	**(N41)**	**(N26)**
	Schizophrenia	43	76
	Affective psychoses	8	15
	Neuroses	28	9
	Personality disorders	19	0
	Epilepsy	2	0

*Diagnosis not known in the case of 4 hostel and 13 group home residents

1.9	**Length of present residence**	**(N45)**	**(N39)**
	Less than 1 year	67	47
	Less than 2 years	22	0
	Less than 5 years	11	43
	5 + years	0	10

	1.10 **Attitude to leaving**		
	Wants to stay	59	73
	Wants to return to hospital	0	3
	Wants to leave	41	24

APPENDIX 2

Differences on Social Performance Schedule

		Hostels (N45)	Group Homes (N39)
2.1	**Demanding behaviour**	%	%
	1 Seldom or never	39	45
	2 Sometimes	36	55
	3 Frequently	25	0

(p < .009)

2.2	**Behavioural instability**		
	1 Marked fluctuation	44	6
	2 Little change	56	94

(p < .001)

2.3	**Social acceptability of manners**		
	1 Markedly unacceptable	25	6
	2 Occasional problems	61	87
	3 Acceptable manners	14	6

(p < .042)

2.4	**Bizarre behaviour**		
	1 Seldom or never	13	3
	2 Sometimes	56	90
	3 Frequently	31	7

(p < .005)

2.5	**Overall degree of handicap**		
	1 Severe and lasting impairment	13	48
	2 Some improvement likely but will remain impaired	64	29
	3 Little permanent impairment	22	23

(p < .001)

	Hostels (N45)	Group Homes (N39)
2.6 Likelihood of successful resettlement	%	%
1 Permanent shelter probably needed	19	74
2 Eventually will not need shelter but unlikely to achieve full and active social life	52	7
3 Should achieve full independence	29	19

$$(p < .000)$$

APPENDIX 3

Moos Perceived Social Environment Scales

Table 3.1 summarises the differences between hostels, group homes, and hotels, as measured by the Moos scales. There are 10 scales, each of six items which can be rated as present (1) or absent (0), so that the range of scores on any one scale is 0-6. These scores were grouped as follows: low (0-2); medium (3 or 4); high (5 or 6). The percentages in these categories are presented separately for the hostels, group homes, and hotels, in the table. A brief explanation of each scale follows. For details, see Moos (1974).

Relationship dimensions

1. Involvement. A measure of how actively and energetically patients become involved in the day-to-day functioning of the unit.

2. Support. A measure of how helpful and supportive residents are towards each other, how well staff understand residents' needs, and how supportive staff are towards residents.

3. Spontaneity. A measure of the extent to which the environment encourages residents to act openly and to express freely their feelings towards other residents and towards staff.

Treatment dimensions

4. Autonomy. A measure of how self-sufficient and independent residents are encouraged to be in their personal affairs and in their relationship with staff, and of how much responsibility and self-direction residents are encouraged to exercise.

5. Practical orientation. A measure of the extent to which the residents' environment is oriented towards preparing them for living independently in the community by encouraging them to cook, clean and shop for themselves.

6. Personal problem orientation. A measure of the extent to which patients are encouraged to be concerned with their social and psychological problems, and to seek to understand them through openly talking to other residents and staff about themselves and their past.

7. Freedom of expression of anger or hostility. A measure of the extent to which a resident is allowed and encouraged to argue with other residents and with staff, and to become openly angry.

Organisational dimensions

8. Routine and order. A measure of the importance of order in the setting, in terms of residents (their personal appearance), staff (what they do to encourage order) and the setting itself (how well it is kept).

9. Programme clarity. A measure of the extent to which the resident knows what to expect in the day-to-day routine of the setting, how explicit its rules or expectations are.

10. Staff control. A measure of the extent to which staff restrict residents – the strictness and severity of the sanctions operating in the setting concerned.

Table 3.1

Scale	Hostels			Group Homes		
	Low	Medium	High	Low	Medium	High
	%	%	%	%	%	%
Involvement	23	57	20	12	55	33
Support	9	49	42	8	50	42
Spontaneity	31	47	22	32	47	21
Autonomy* (.0000)	29	38	33	0	12	88
Practical Orientation* (.0015)	32	61	7	6	69	25
Personal problem	22	47	30	37	41	22
Anger and hostility* (.0023)	44	44	12	78	22	0
Order and organisation	11	49	40	15	58	27
Programme clarity	13	62	24	8	55	37
Staff control* (.0139)	37	37	26	65	27	8

* = significant difference between hostels and group homes (Chi-squared)

APPENDIX 4

Decision-Making Schedule

The schedule contains 23 situations likely to occur in any community caring for the 'adult mentally ill'. Each resident was asked how a decision would be reached as to how to cope with the situation. The three alternatives presented were: (1) that, on the whole, residents decide; (2) that a process of consultation goes on, resulting in a joint decision; (3) that, on the whole, staff members decide. A distinction can be made between eight 'management' decisions (e.g. whether a resident in relapse should return to hospital, who should pay 'phone bills, whether to admit a new resident, etc.), and fifteen decisions involving problems of daily living (e.g. what time residents should get up in the morning, how to organise house 'socials', what to have for dinner, etc.) or problems of resident behaviour (e.g. when one resident is physically violent to another, or when a resident sits about completely unoccupied).

Table 4.1 summarises the data on all 23 decisions and Table 4.2 the data on eight management decisions.

Table 4.1
Decision-making as reported by residents

Unit	No. of Residents	No. of Residents responding	Decision taken by: Residents %	Joint %	Staff %
Hostel 1	6	4	25	52	23
Hostel 2	14	12	25	42	33
Hostel 3	19	14	15	17	68
Preparation Unit	6	4	39	21	40
Self-care annexe	7	6	50	17	33
Hostel 4	9	7	24	16	60
All hostels	61	47	36	26	47
Network 1	12	10	52	23	25
Network 2	19	12	42	16	42
Network 3	19	17	65	21	14
All group homes	50	39	55	20	25

N.B. Each resident responded to 23 items. Thus the 47 residents of hostels responded to 47 x 23 = 1081 items. The percentages shown relate to the total number of items responded to per group.

Table 4.2

Management decisions as reported by residents

Unit	No. of Residents	No. of Residents responding	Decision taken by: Residents %	Joint %	Staff %
Hostel 1	6	4	9	44	47
Hostel 2	14	12	16	42	42
Hostel 3	19	14	1	8	91
Preparation Unit	6	4	12	19	69
Self-care annexe	7	6	27	17	56
Hostel 4	9	7	7	11	82
All hostels	61	47	11	22	67
Network 1	12	10	28	24	48
Network 2	19	12	17	13	70
Network 3	19	17	53	21	26
All group homes	50	39	37	19	44

N.B. Each resident responded to 8 management items.

APPENDIX 5

The problems of behaviour most commonly described by staff in response to the Social Performance Schedule are listed, in overall rank order, in Table 5.1, together with their rank order in each of the four hostels. Table 5.2 shows the types of interventions used by staff in order to try to help residents with these problems.

Table 5.1

Frequency of occurrence of problem behaviours

Problem behaviour	Overall frequency %	Rank order Hostel			
		1	2	3	4
1. Avoidance of social contact	16	2	2	1	2.5
2. Poor performance of hostel and personal chores	13	4.5	4	2	1
3. Over-assertion	11	10	1	5.5	2.5
4. Overdependence	10	10	3	7.5	5.5
5. Under-involvement	7	2	6	9.5	10.0
6. Work difficulties	7	4.5	8.5	4	8
7. Anxiety about leaving	7	7	8.5	3	8
8. Inconsistency	6	12	11	5.5	4
9. Low self-esteem	6	7	11	7.5	5.5
10. Depression	5	7	6	9.5	11
11. Under-assertion	5	2	11	12	12
12. Inappropriate social behaviour	5	10	6	11	8
Other	4	—	—	—	—

Table 5.2

Frequency of use of various types of intervention by staff

Type of intervention	Overall frequency %	Frequency in			
		Hostel 1 %	Hostel 2 %	Hostel 3 %	Hostel 4 %
No intervention made	24	17	16	29	33
Non-technical	52	50	51	59	47
Technical	25	33	33	12	20

APPENDIX 6

Staff time available per week per resident
in hostels compared with group homes

Setting	No. of staff	Total staff time hours	No. of residents	Staff time per resident hours
Hostel 1	3	120	5	24.0
Hostel 2	5	200	12	16.6
Hostel 3	5	200	30	6.6
Hostel 4	3	120	7	17.1
All hostels	16	640	54	11.9
Network 1	6*	2.0	12	0.2
Network 2†	5**	2.7	27	0.1
Network 3	4***	1.3	19	0.1
All group homes	15	6.0	58	0.1

† including 2 hotels

* One social worker plus one volunteer per home

** One co-ordinator (employment and accommodation officer) plus one nurse/O.T. per home

*** Two area-based, and two hospital based social workers, one of whom supervised two homes

APPENDIX 7

Comparison of hostel and group home costs 1975-76

	Hostel 1		Hostel 2		Hostel 3		Hostel 4		Group Home Network 2	
Average number of residents	7		14		26		7		16	
Number of resident weeks	364		720		1301		376		832	
Percentage occupancy	100%		69%		78%		66%		94%	
Cost per resident week	£	p	£	p	£	p	£	p	£	p
Expenditure										
Employees (wages, salaries and car allowance)	35	47	39	19	21	40	50	17	1	08
Premises (furniture, fuels, light, rates, etc.)	12	77	8	14	12	01	11	54	3	54
Supplies & Services (equipment, provisions, laundry, etc.)	7	44	8	36	8	22	8	26	–	–
Miscellaneous expenses (stationery, telephone)	4	18	1	78	0	97	2	00	0	29
Debt charges	9	04	13	69	10	96	1	85	1	09
Total expenditure	68	90	71	71	53	56	73	82	6	00
Income										
Staff board and lodging	0	68	1	11	–	–	1	56	–	–
Resident rents	9	26	8	74	10	65	11	30	4	00
Miscellaneous	3	85	0	11	0	95	0	08	0	89
Total income	13	79	9	96	11	60	12	94	4	89
Cost per resident week	55	11	61	21	41	96	60	88	1	11
Wage-Net cost ratio	64%		64%		51%		82%		96%	
Income-cost ratio	20%		14%		22%		18%		81%	

References

Creer, C. (1975), Living with schizophrenia. *Social Work Today, 6,* 2-7.

Creer, C. and Wing, J. K. (1974), *Schizophrenia at Home.* National Schizophrenia Fellowship, 29, Victoria Road, Surbiton, Surrey KT6 4JT.

Department of Health & Social Security (1975), *Better Services for the Mentally Ill.* Cmnd 6233. London: HMSO.

Hewett, S., Ryan, P. and Wing, J. K. (1975), Living without the mental hospitals. *J. soc. Policy, 4,* 391-404.

Leach, J. and Wing, J. K. (1979a), Action research with the St. Mungo Community. To be published.

Leach, J. and Wing, J. K. (1979b), *Helping Destitute Men.* London: Tavistock. To be published.

Mann, S. and Cree, W. (1976), 'New' long-stay psychiatric patients: A national sample of 15 mental hospitals in England and Wales, 1972/3. *Psychol. Med. 6,* 603-16.

Mann, S. and Sproule, J. (1972), Reasons for a six months stay. In: *Evaluating a Community Psychiatric Service.* Eds: Wing, J. K. and Hailey, A. M. London: Oxford University Press.

Moos, R. H. (1974), *Evaluating Treatment Environments.* New York: Wiley.

Ryan, P. (1979), New forms of residential care for the mentally ill. In: *Community Care for the Mentally Disabled.* Eds: J. K. Wing and Rolf Olsen. London: Oxford University Press.

Ryan, P. and Hewett, S. H. (1976), A pilot study of hostels for the mentally ill. *Social Work Today, 6,* 25, 774-778.

Seelye, A. (1976), Hostels for the mentally ill in ordinary houses, Medical Architecture Research Unit.

Tidmarsh, D. and Wood, S. (1972), Psychiatric aspects of destitution: the Camberwell Reception Centre. In: Wing and Hailey, *op. cit.,* chapter 21, and Report to DHSS.

Vaughn, C. E. and Leff, J. P. (1976), The influence of family and social factors on the course of psychiatric illness. *Brit. J. Psychiat. 129,* 125-137.

Wing, J. K. (1974), Sheltered environments for the psychiatrically handicapped. In: *Providing a Comprehensive District Psychiatric Service for the Adult Mentally Ill.* DHSS: Reports on Health and Social Subjects, No. 8. London: HMSO.

Wing, J. K. (1977), The management of Schizophrenia in the community. In: *Psychiatric Medicine.* Ed: Usdin, G. New York: Brunner, Mazel.

Wing, J. K. and Brown, G. W. (1970), *Institutionalism and Schizophrenia.* London: Cambridge University Press.

Wing, J. K. and Leach, J. (1979), The rehabilitation and resettlement of destitute men. To be published.

PART FIVE

DAY CARE

6: Psychiatric Day Hospital Care

Christine Hassall

Summary

This chapter traces the development of psychiatric day care from the opening of the first day hospital in this country in 1946 to the present day. It discusses the various advantages which have been attributed to day care and the diversity of programmes in different day hospital settings. The original concept of day care as a short term measure has had to be modified. With the reduction of psychiatric beds, many severely handicapped patients receive most, if not all, of their psychiatric treatment while still living in the community. Excerpts from two studies illustrate the build up of long stay (12 months or more) patients and underlines the difficulties that this can create. If the long term severely handicapped patient is to be treated in the day hospital setting it is necessary to be realistic both in our goals and the time scale over which it will take to achieve them. The dangers of creating a two tier system are emphasised and the need for adequate staffing, suitable premises and active programmes for those in long term day hospital care stressed.

Day hospital care is potentially the most intensive form of care available to psychiatric patients living outside the hospital; it is the corner-stone of community based psychiatric services.

Background to the day hospital movement

Just over 30 years ago, in 1946, Joshua Bierer opened the Social Psychotherapy Centre, later to change its venue and become the now well known Malborough Day Hospital.[1] This centre treated a wide range of mental illness using methods based on the principles of social psychiatry. Although the venture was watched with interest it was regarded as largely experimental and it was five years before a second psychiatric day hospital was opened in Bristol. By 1959 however there were 38,[2] in 1966 there were 65, and by 1972 this number had more than doubled to reach 145.[3,4]

Although the first day hospital was opened in 1946 the concept of day patients was not new. As Farndale[2] comments, many large mental hospitals had been supporting day patients for a number of years. These were almost

111

always discharged inpatients who attended on an informal basis usually returning to their former wards and sharing the inpatient routine.

What was new was the concept of day hospital care as a separate entity, a therapeutic tool in its own right, and with special advantages.

The advantages of day hospital care

The Ministry of Health (as it then was) expressed an interest in day hospitals in the Report of the Central Health Service Council in 1951. The function of the day hospital had previously been examined by the Standing Mental Health Advisory Committee which put forward several points in their favour, not least of which was, that day hospitals could save inpatient beds and therefore reduce costs. Another advantage cited was that psychiatric day patient care might prove a more acceptable form of care than inpatient treatment and thus encourage patients to be treated earlier than might otherwise have been the case if admission to mental hospital was the only option.

Further reports from the Ministry commented favourably on psychiatric day hospitals (1953, 1955 and 1956). After The Hospital Plan (1962)[5] was published, more emphasis was laid on the concept of community care and supporting facilities.[6,7] Thus the Ministry, now the Department of Health and Social Security, saw the advantages of day hospital care from the early days of the movement, though in the 1950s the emphasis of their reports was on saving beds and therefore money, the reduction of overcrowding, and prevention of admission, while their later publications stressed the importance of day care as part of community psychiatric service with full supporting facilities. The more recent " Better Services for the Mentally Ill" has put forward the idea that in future as many as half the available day hospital places will be occupied by inpatients thus bringing the inpatient into the day hospital as an early step towards returning to the community.

The Department of Health was not alone in its appreciation of the advantages of day hospital care, psychiatrists also recognised its particular merits. Bierer[9] placed great importance on avoiding the 'shock' of admission, stressing also that day care tended to minimise the excessive dependence which an inpatient so easily develops. Harris[10] in his decription of the Bethlem and Maudsley day hospitals declared that the advantages of day hospital treatment are economic and social, also underlining the importance (particularly for the middle-aged and the elderly) of not nursing the patient away from his home. Sheldon and May,[11] writing of the Croydon Day Hospital, whose parent hospital is Warlingham Park, point out that:—

112

"the therapeutic atmosphere derives not only from its easily accessible location in the community (both for patients *and* their relatives) but also from the special status of those who attend."

They comment further that a patient who lives in the community can bring a better contribution to group discussions than those confined to a hospital. Whitehead[12] in his book "In the Service of Old Age" underlines the advantages of day hospital care for the elderly stressing the importance of preventing admission and the relief often afforded to caring relatives. Bennett[13] emphasises that:—

"The day hospital patient is able to obtain help as a sick person while he still retains something of his status as a husband or father at home. . . . The day hospital plays an important part in the patient's clinical rehabilitation by neither removing him from his role in society, nor forcing him to play a totally deviant role".

Parallel with this increasing understanding of the advantages of day hospital care during the 1950s and 1960s came the movement to reduce overcrowding in the large mental hospitals where conditions in the 'back wards' were often far from satisfactory. Often larger mental hospitals saw day care as an alternative for many of these long stay patients.

As early as 1961 Farndale[2] noted the diversity of day hospitals both in their physical conditions and in their aims. Some were accommodated in wards no longer used for inpatients, others in new premises built in mental hospital grounds. A few isolated hospitals in rural sites sought more convenient premises in the population centres they served. The treatment programmes adopted were equally varied, some were run on therapeutic community principles, others were more concerned with physical treatments and traditional occupational therapy. Most recognised that the discipline of the inpatient ward was unsuitable in such a setting and might even defeat the re-establishment of the patient's confidence and his ability to organise himself outside the hospital setting. A considerable diversity of aims and facilities still remains today, this is highlighted in the study of day hospital care in Birmingham[14,15] carried out by the author and two colleagues in 1968.

Psychiatric day care in Birmingham

A census was made of all patients attending the psychiatric day hospital facilities in the City of Birmingham during the course of one week. The facilities comprised four large day hospitals (342, 104, 85 and 52 patients respectively) and three small units (26, 19, and 19 patients). Thus 583

Birmingham day patients attended large day hospitals attached to traditional mental hospitals and 64 attended small day hospitals attached to small psychiatric inpatient units. These two types of day hospital demonstrated the possible divergency of day care facilities in many aspects; physical accommodation, staffing, patients' programme and the characteristics of the patients attending.

The physical accommodation for the day patients in the large day hospitals varied from Nissen huts and prefabricated buildings, to converted inpatient wards, to purpose built accommodation (though at that time the latter accounted for a very small section of patients): the small day hospitals occupied relatively modern buildings, one was a converted mansion house standing in spacious grounds and one had been opened less than a decade. The staff/patient ratios were much more favourable in the small hospitals – for example, three nurses and an assistant for 19 patients – than in the large day hospitals where two nurses might look after 60 long term patients with schizophrenia. A few active and co-operative patients attended occupational or industrial therapy in the large hospitals but it was clear that the majority of patients spent their time unoccupied, sitting on the wards, rarely communicating with each other or the staff, though they would do simple tasks about the ward if asked. All the small day hospitals had a daily programme of group meetings and other activities and the greater part of the patients' day was taken up by these.

It was, however, the characteristics of the patients attending these two types of day hospital which most dramatically differentiated them. In the large day hospitals only a quarter of the patients were less than 45 years old, while a third were 65 years and over; in the small hospitals, three-quarters of the patients were under 45 years of age and only three per cent (two patients) were elderly. With regard to diagnosis 43 per cent of those in the large day hospitals were suffering from schizophrenia or other affective psychosis while only 12 per cent of patients in the small hospitals came into this category. A further 14 per cent of those in the large hospitals were diagnosed as having senile or other organic psychosis while there were no such patients in the small hospitals. When the patients' records were examined to determine the length of time that they had been in day care almost half (46 per cent) of those attending the large hospitals had been attending for a year or more (some for as long as four years) while none of their counterparts in the small hospitals had attended for this length of time, and 87 per cent had been in day care for less than six months. About half these long stay patients were elderly; most were suffering from schizophrenia or other affective disorder.

Patients were followed up in the day hospitals for one year. The mean attendance rate for those who had already been attending for more than a year at the census date was between three and four days. This rate of attendance showed only a small decline over the follow up year.

This study emphasises the need to be realistic about day care. It has been described as 'a transitional or intermediary stage between home and hospital' and certainly the most usual concept of day care is treatment lasting weeks or months rather than years. Clearly, for a large proportion of day patients in Birmingham in 1968 it was neither transitional nor intermediary. Furthermore, for a substantial proportion of patients, day care was differentiated from care on the back wards only by the fact that they lived outside the hospital.

Psychiatric day care in Powick Hospital catchment area

Some 40 miles south-west of Birmingham lies Powick Hospital. This mental hospital and its catchment area have been chosen by D.H.S.S. as the site of a test-bed, or prototype community based psychiatric service, known as the Worcester Development Project.[16] Under this project, first mooted in 1968,[17] it is proposed to:—

"replace an old isolated mental hospital of some 949 beds* and very irregularly developed community facilities by a comprehensive service comprising departments in district general hospitals placed in urban centres, with outpatient departments, day hospitals and special facilities for children and adolescents; and community facilities including day centres, hostels, residential homes for the elderly and a full system of social work support".

Under the Development Project, Powick Hospital, currently with about 450 beds, will be replaced by two general hospital psychiatric units. (A residual group of long stay patients will remain at the old hospital but admissions will cease as the new units open.) The two new units sited at Worcester and Kidderminster will have 160 and 50 inpatient beds respectively.

At present there are approximately 100 day hospital places at Powick Hospital (the only source of this type of care presently available in the catchment area); these will be replaced by 160 and 80 places at the new

*In 1968 when the Feasibility Study was carried out.

inpatient units and, in addition, 20 places each will be provided at two day hospitals in Malvern and Evesham. When the project is completed therefore there will be a total of 280 places. It has been proposed[8] that up to half the available day places may be occupied by inpatients. However, since there will be no inpatients at Evesham or Malvern this should only mean a reduction of about 110-120 places between Kidderminster and Worcester. There will be a net gain of 60-70 places, furthermore this form of care will be available at four urban centres in the catchment area instead of confined to a single somewhat inconvenient site. Thus day hospital care assumes a major role in the new community psychiatric service.

Although, at Powick, patients had attended for day care on an informal basis for many years, (usually returning to their former inpatient wards), the first day hospital in separate accommodation was opened in the summer of 1972. A second day hospital, intended for elderly psychiatric patients, was opened six months later, though some elderly patients, particularly if they are not physically frail, may attend with the younger patients. These day hospitals are housed in wards which are no longer used for inpatients.

With the Birmingham Study in mind and the opportunity to monitor the Powick day hospitals almost from inception, an ongoing study of patients in this type of care and their patterns of service use was set up as part of the evaluation of the Worcester Development Project.

In order to examine the development of these day hospitals and the characteristics of the patients using them, all patients on the books on the 1st January each year are drawn from the psychiatric case register to form a yearly cohort. The characteristics of the four cohorts presently available have been analysed with particular attention to any changes in diagnostic categories, age, or length of stay. The computerised record does not distinguish between the two day hospitals and the findings are therefore given for both combined.

There are 86 patients in the 1973 cohort and 103 in each of the other years.

Table 1 (see page 117) illustrates the sex and age group distribution of the cohorts. There has been a marked rise in the population of male patients attending for day hospital care. In 1973, males made up 27 per cent of the total, this increased through 33 and 40 to 43 per cent in 1976. The proportion of elderly day patients also increased over the first three cohorts (32, 34 and 47 per cent) but fell slightly in 1976 to 44 per cent.

116

Table 1
Day patient cohorts by sex and age group
(per cent in brackets)

age group	year of cohort											
	1973			1974			1975			1976		
	male	female	total	male	female	total	male	female	total	male	female	total
< 45 years	8	9	17 (20)	10	12	22 (21)	10	10	20 (19)	14	6	20 (19)
45 < 65 years	9	32	41 (48)	16	30	46 (45)	15	20	35 (34)	17	21	38 (37)
65 years and over	6	22	28 (32)	8	27	35 (34)	16	32	48 (47)	13	32	45 (44)
total	23 (27)	63 (73)	86 (100)	34 (33)	69 (67)	103 (100)	41 (40)	62 (60)	103 (100)	44 (43)	59 (57)	103 (100)

Table 2

Day patient cohorts — diagnostic groups

(per cent in brackets)

diagnostic group	year of cohort			
	1973	1974	1975	1976
Senile and pre-senile dementia	9 (10.5)	8 (8)	12 (12)	6 (6)
Schizophrenia and other psychosis	31 (36)	42 (41)	40 (39)	42 (41)
All neurosis	15 (17)	18 (17)	16 (15)	20 (19)
Depression N.O.S.	22 (26)	20 (19)	24 (23)	22 (21)
Other	9 (10.5)	15 (15)	11 (11)	13 (13)
total	86 (100)	103 (100)	103 (100)	103 (100)

The diagnostic groupings are shown in Table 2. The 'schizophrenia and other psychosis' group increased over the first two cohorts (36 to 41 per cent), fell slightly in the third (39 per cent) and regained its former level in the 1976 cohort (41 per cent). Senile and pre-senile dementia accounted for only a small proportion of the patients in any cohort but was at its lowest (6 per cent) in the 1976 cohort.

Table 3

Day patients — length of stay in day care

(per cent in brackets)

length of stay	year of cohort			
	1973	1974	1975	1976
Under 1 month	10 (12)	1 (1)	8 (8)	10 (10)
1 month < 6 months	32 (37)	44 (43)	32 (31)	26 (25)
6 months < 1 year	34 (39)	25 (24)	12 (12)	20 (19)
1 year and over	10 (12)	33 (32)	51 (49)	47 (46)
total	86 (100)	103 (100)	103 (100)	103 (100)

Patients' records were examined to establish how long they had been in day hospital care (Table 3). Day care was considered to be continuous even though patients received inpatient care if day care continued up to the time they were admitted and was resumed immediately after discharge. (In some cases patients continued to attend while they were on the inpatient wards). The percentage of patients in day care for one year or more increases rapidly through the first three cohorts, 12, 32 and 49 per cent, falling slightly in 1976 to 46 per cent. The 'long stay' patients in the 1973 cohort were those who had been attending informally before the separate day hospitals opened. However, after only three years, half the day patients are long stay.

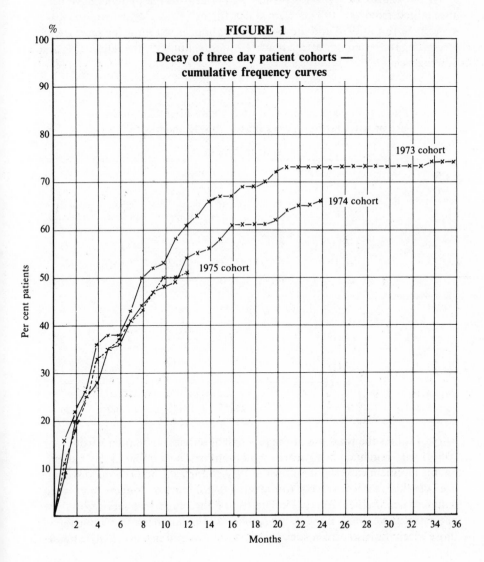

FIGURE 1

Decay of three day patient cohorts — cumulative frequency curves

1973 cohort

1974 cohort

1975 cohort

Per cent patients

Months

The three earlier cohorts were followed up until December 1975. Figure 1, using cumulative frequency curves, illustrate the decay of these cohorts. The 1973 cohort shows the greatest rate of decay with 61 per cent of the patients having been discharged at the end of 12 months compared with 54 and 51 per cent respectively for the two later cohorts.

At the end of two years a further 12 per cent of the patients have been discharged from the 1973 cohort and a further 15 per cent from the 1974 cohort. Both the 1973 and the 1974 cohorts appear to follow the same trend, beginning to flatten out after about 16 months, but with the later curve at a lower level.

Table 4

**Patients in each cohort still in day care after 12 months —
use of psychiatric services during this 12 months follow-up**

(per cent in brackets)

	1973 (n=33)		1974 (n=47)		1975 (n=50)	
	no. of patients	mean days/ contacts	no. of patients	mean days/ contacts	no. of patients	mean days/ contacts
IP care	6 (18)	49	13 (28)	24	13 (26)	33
DP care	33 (100)	126	47 (100)	139	50 (100)	122
OP visits	5 (15)	10	2 (4)	1	1 (2)	1
Social worker visits	4 (12)	3	4 (8)	1	10 (20)	6
Community nurse visits	3 (19)	1	7 (15)	3	14 (28)	3
Psychiatrist home visit	1 (3)	1	—	—	3 (6)	1
No. in DP care only	16 (48)	112	25 (53)	129	24 (48)	120

Table 4 shows the total use of the psychiatric services by patients from each cohort who remained in day care for 12 months. The number of day patients having inpatient care was least for the 1973 cohort, although those who made use of this service stayed (on average) for rather longer than their counterparts in 1974 and 1975. The use of the outpatient service by these patients was minimal in the last two cohorts. The number and proportion of those receiving visits from social workers or community psychiatric nurses was also increased through the three years. The proportion of the long stay patients who did not make use of any other psychiatric service was just under half for the 1973 and 1975 cohorts and just over half for the middle year.

An interesting sub-group of 22 patients from the 1973 cohort was still in day care after three years. Half of these patients were elderly and half (some of them elderly) were suffering from schizophrenia or other psychosis. The mean number of days attended (per patient in the group) fell from 140 in 1973 to 130 in 1974 but remained virtually the same at 129 days in the third year. The patients in this group who were elderly had lower means for each yeas (119, 98 and 106) than those who were aged less than 65 years (161, 162 and 152).

In summary, each of the yearly cohorts examined in this study had substantial proportions of patients who were elderly, and also of those suffering from schizophrenia or other affective psychosis. Long stay patients accounted for approximately half of the third cohort and 46 per cent in the last cohort available. Most significant is the small group of patients, (accounting for about one-fifth of the available day places) who have been in day care for three years. Not only do many of this group bear the hallmark of the long stay patient i.e. advancing age and/or schizophrenia or affective psychosis, but their rate of attendance, which is frequent, shows little change over the three years. Considering the relatively short time day care has been available at Powick Hospital there is a substantial proportion of 'long stay' patients, and some silting up of the day hospital facilities.

It might be predicted that long term attenders will stabilise at around half the yearly cohort. The changes in service provision arising from the continued implementation of the Development Project make any such prediction problematical as it is almost impossible to judge the effect of these changes. For example, two new local authority day centres have been open for rather less than 18 months. These are an innovation in the area and as yet it is too early to determine what types of patient will, in the long term, be most likely to use them. A small proportion of those who attended during 1977 had also received day hospital care suggesting that there is some possibility that the day centres may affect the length of attendance in the day hospital. The team of community psychiatric nurses has also increased over the past three years and this too may affect the number of day hospital attenders. The most fundamental change to take place will be the opening of the two new psychiatric inpatient units and the transfer of day hospital care to these units and, though somewhat later, to the two small day hospitals. This seems likely to lead to some re-appraisal of existing patients and policies, particularly as substantial numbers of inpatients will be sharing the accommodation at the two largest day hospitals.

Even more difficult to anticipate are the effects of removing the day hospitals from the site of the mental hospital and providing this form of care in four centres in the catchment area. It becomes, at once, more accessible and perhaps more acceptable to an increased number of patients. It is possible that, if a shorter travelling time allows a patient to attend more frequently, his course of treatment may be shortened. This may indeed be the case for some patients but the continued high frequency attendance of many long term patients both in the Birmingham day hospitals and at Powick does not encourage this view in regard to the more severely disabled. Overall, it is expected that the number of day patients will increase to fill the available places. Whether this silting up process will be re-established remains to be seen but since it is clear that a substantial proportion of day patients require long term care, it does not seem likely that this trend will disappear unless these patients receive their care from one of the new or increased resources described above. As Baldwin[18] commented:—

> "neither the mental hospital nor any other part of the complex of services can function independently, as if the others did not exist; . . . this view of the actual organisation of psychiatric services implies that alteration of the function of one part will affect the function of other parts and the whole will behave as a single system".

The cost of day care at Powick Hospital

The costs of day care are in general lower than the costs of inpatient care solely because patients do not usually attend for a full week. In Powick Hospital costing returns for 1975/6 the average cost per day patient attendance is given as £8.67. This figure is, however, computed in a somewhat bizarre fashion, and it was considered necessary to build up an estimate of the costs of the day hospital from the costs of its constituents. This method yielded a figure of £9.74.

All except a very few patients are brought to the day hospital by ambulance. In order to compute the ambulance cost it was necessary to count the vehicle miles involved in the six or seven double round trips made daily in order to carry patients to the day hospital, and to apply average revenue costs, depreciation and capital costs to this mileage, which was then divided by the average number of daily attendances. In 1975/6 revenue costs for the ambulance service in the Hereford and Worcester AHA were 86.4p per

vehicle mile. Capital costs were estimated separately from a knowledge of the operational 'write off' mileage and the costs of new sitting case vehicles. The estimate is 8.8p per vehicle mile, giving a total of 95.2p. Weekly mileage for day patients is approximately 1,575 miles and, the average daily attendance is 48. The cost per attendance is, therefore, £6.25.

Total public support for patients attending the day hospital is not confined to the supply of resources by the health service. Social security payments are made, and these can be substantial for single persons living on their own. (They can also, of course, be substantial for persons with dependents, but in this case admission as an inpatient does not radically reduce entitlement in the same way as admission of a person without dependents.) Invalidity benefit, at 13.30 per week, compares with £2.65 inpatient 'pocket money' for long stay patients, and £8 for those who have been in hospital for less than a year. Supplementary benefit can raise the difference between inpatient and day patient receipts to a figure of around £17.50 per week. It was not possible to collect information concerning actual receipts of any of the cohorts studied, so a conservative guessed figure of £5 per week *above the social security cost of inpatient stay* has been entered. In this way a statement of the absolute level of support is avoided, and the total figures estimated remain directly comparable with average hospital inpatient stay cost figures.

The cost of an attendance was, therefore, £15.99 and the weekly cost of an individual's care derived by multiplying number of attendances in a week by this figure should be augmented by £5.

Figure 2 shows the distribution of weekly costs of patients attending the day hospital. Each cost corresponds to a number of attendances, 1-5 per week, and the distribution is based upon the attendance pattern during the first week of June 1974. During the same period, the cost of inpatient care ranged from £60-£120, depending upon ward, the long-stay wards being the cheapest. Figures 3 (a-c) show the distribution of estimated annual costs of support (1975/6 prices) for those patients from the 1973, 1974 and 1975 cohorts who were still in day care after a year. In some cases (32 out of 129) these patients were admitted to inpatient care for a mean 32 days, and for them the costs of inpatient stay have been added, lest a misleading impression should be given that the overall costs of care for some patients are less than they actually are.

The average cost for three years care for each member of the group of 22 patients who attended continuously for a further length of time from January 1973 was £7,300. An element of this was incurred by admission to inpatient care, but the average of five days each per year was less than the average over all the members of all the cohorts.

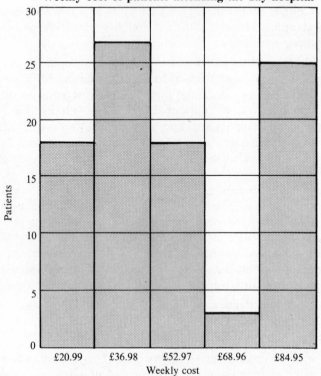

FIGURE 2
Weekly cost of patients attending the day hospital

Patients (y-axis: 0, 5, 10, 15, 20, 25, 30)

Weekly cost: £20.99, £36.98, £52.97, £68.96, £84.95

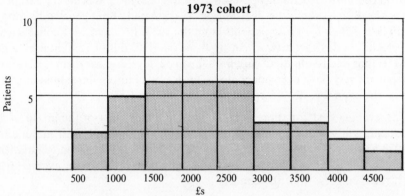

FIGURE 3a
Estimated annual costs of long term day patients
1973 cohort

Patients (y-axis: 5, 10)

£s: 500, 1000, 1500, 2000, 2500, 3000, 3500, 4000, 4500

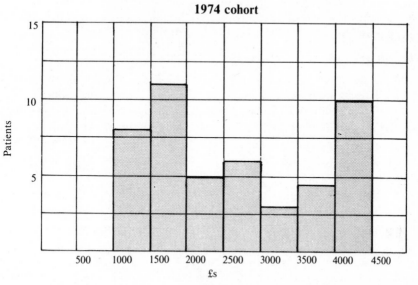

FIGURE 3b
Estimated annual costs of long term patients
1974 cohort

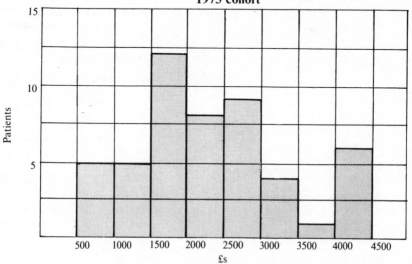

FIGURE 3c
Estimated annual costs of long term patients
1975 cohort

Approximately a third of the costs of day care at Powick Hospital is due to the cost of transporting patients by ambulance which is of course related to the distances travelled. When day hospital care is dispersed to four centres in the catchment area the distances involved should be substantially less and this element of the overall cost may be reduced.

The present state of the day hospital movement

The early years of the expansion of day hospital care also saw the movement to discharge considerable numbers of patients from the back wards of the large mental hospitals in an attempt to alleviate overcrowding. It was hoped that if these patients could be dispersed new treatment programme and a community care approach would prevent them being replaced. Problems of institutionalisation would be a thing of the past save for those remaining long-stay patients who, by reasons of age or disability, were unsuitable for discharge from inpatient care. The idea that the day hospital would be a stage in a short term treatment programme was encouraged.

By the early 1970s however, it was clear that in spite of these measures long term patients were in fact still accumulating on the wards though at a much slower rate than in former days,[19] and furthermore, long-stay patients were also to be found in the day hospitals.[15,20] As a result of what a leading article in the British Medical Journal[21] acidly described as a 'sociological conjuring trick' long stay patients had in some degree disappeared from the long stay wards only to reappear in the day hospitals.

The concept of day care solely as a short term treatment facility, aiding early discharge or preventing admission has had to be modified. It is not that day care has failed in these aims but that it is now also an important resource in the treatment of long-stay patients, a role not originally forseen.

The Birmingham study illustrated only too clearly the dangers of a two tier system developing. At one end of the continuum, small well staffed day hospitals with active treatment programmes and young patients with relatively good prognosis; at the other, large day hospitals with poor staff patient ratio, the majority of the patients middle-aged or elderly, suffering from severely disabling psychiatric disorder. A further difference was the allocation of medical time. In the small hospitals medical staff were present at least part of every day. In the large hospitals they came, in the main, for an occasional review of the patients or in an emergency; they were not involved with ward activities. This position arose because no medical time was specifically allocated to the day hospital, it was simply 'run in' with other responsibilities.

In many areas, apart from having a separate day hospital for the elderly (and this is not always the case), all patients attend the same day hospital. The success of this may well depend on the number of long term attenders, whether these are 'new long stay' or, perhaps more difficult to integrate, patients with long standing psychiatric disorder. If there is a substantial proportion of such patients the treatment programme may have to be modified.

Where day hospitals cater for short or medium stay cases treatment programmes are usually directed towards giving patients insights into their problem and difficulties, relieving symptoms, exploring relationships and helping them to take up their lives more fully in family and community. Such techniques as group therapy, behaviour therapy and social skills training may be available as well as medication and psychiatric support. Social workers and psychologists are often involved in day hospital programmes. In addition, such activities as relaxation classes, drama reading, cookery and occupational therapy may also fill the timetable.

In day hospitals, usually attached to large mental hospitals, where there large numbers of long term patients the therapeutic goals are more modest and the time in which they may be achieved much longer. Many such units make use of occupational therapy or simple industrial therapy for which small payments are received. Ward meetings are held and patients encouraged to discuss their problem on a practical level. Even in these hospitals there is usually a small nucleus of patients for whom long term rehabilitation may result in some hope of employment or perhaps resettlement in the community with little or no support. For many however, even this is a distant, perhaps unattainable prospect. Considerable support will always be needed if they are to live outside the hospital and for many this will be provided by day hospital care. The problem is to design a programme which will occupy these patients developing small skills, helping them to communicate and generally improving the quality of their lives. The benefits of such a programme accrue not only to the patients but to the staff. An active programme with realistic aims is good for the morale of all in a unit where success, if measured by discharge, is small.

Day hospitals for the elderly have similar problems; although many of the elderly suffer from psychiatric disorders of later life rather than long standing illness, their age limits the treatment goals that can be set up. However, as with long-stay, programmes are usually oriented towards occupation, developing or restoring social skills and helping the patient towards as full and independent a life as possible.

There are also day hospitals attached to specialist units which treat alcholism or drug addiction or sometimes both. In these, addicts can take their first steps back into the community, with, for them, all its attendant problems and temptation, while receiving substantial psychiatric support.

As more small psychiatric inpatient units are set up with relatively few beds the number of patients in short term day care is likely to increase. From the ranks of these a few will graduate to long term day care but not in sufficient numbers to replace the 'old' long term patients discharged to day care after many years of inpatient care. Also, since the latter have been disadvantaged by institutionalisation while the former have not, the needs of the new long-stay are likely to be different. Christie Brown[22] warns that our view of the number of new chronic patients may be over optimistic pointing out that:—

"it is likely that an increase of psychiatrically ill people in prison, in reception centres and common lodging houses and among the ranks of the destitute homeless may account in part for the smaller number of new chronics in hospital".

This may be the case but it seems likely that such persons would, if they returned to psychiatric care, need a more sheltered environment than the day hospital can offer. However, a further source of increase is the growing numbers of elderly people in the general population which will almost certainly lead to a greater requirement for day hospital places.

Conclusion

Day hospital care has become a major resource in the community based psychiatric services. It seems realistic to plan, not only for short and medium term patients, but also for both the old and the new long-stay in day care: though the new long-stay will be entirely different both in their disabilities and their needs. Increased demand for places is likely to be generated by the reduction of inpatient beds and the growing number of elderly people in the general population. Although different treatment approaches, occupational programmes, and rehabilitative measures are necessary (perhaps in separate facilities) if the full range of patients' needs are to be met, the dangers of creating a two tier system must be recognised. This can only be avoided by adequate staffing and active programmes for those in long term day care.

Acknowledgement

I am indebted to John Stilwell, Research Fellow, Health Services Research Centre, University of Birmingham for the section on the costs of day hospital care at Powick Hospital.

References

1. Bierer, J. (1955), The Day Hospital, Social Welfare, *9,* 172-179.
2. Farndale, J. (1961), *The Day Hospital Movement in Great Britain,* London and Oxford, Pergamon Press.
3. Department of Health and Social Security (1969), A Pilot study of patients attending day hospitals, Statistical Report Series No. 7, London, H.M.S.O.
4. Department of Health and Social Security, (1975) Statistical and Research Report Series No. 10. London, H.M.S.O.
5. Ministry of Health. (1962), A Hospital Plan for England and Wales, Cmnd. 1604, London, H.M.S.O.
6. Ministry of Health. (1964a), *Improving the Effectiveness of Hospitals for the Mentally Ill.* Memorandum H.M., 64,4.
7. Ministry of Health. (1964b), Health and Welfare. *The Development of Community Care,* London, H.M.S.O.
8. Department of Health and Social Security, (1975), *Better Services for the Mentally Ill,* London, H.M.S.O.
9. Bierer, J. (1951), The Day Hospital: *an experiment in Social Psychiatry Synthoanalytic Psychotherapy,* London, H. K. Lewis.
10. Harris, A. (1957), Day Hospitals and Night Hospitals in Psychiatry, Lancet, *i,* 729-730.
11. Sheldon, A. P. and May, A. R. (1967). The Day Hospital in a Comprehensive Psychiatric Service, in *New Aspects of the Mental Health Services,* ed. Freeman, H. and Farndale, J. London and Oxford, Pergamon Press.
12. Whitehead, A. (1970), *In the Service of Old Age,* London, Penguin Books.
13. Bennett, D. H. (1972), Day hospitals, day centres, and work shops in Evaluating a Community Psychiatric Service, *ed.* Wing, J. K. and Hailey, A. M. pub. for the Nuffield Prov. Hosp. Trust, Oxford University Press.
14. Hassall, Christine, Gath, D., and Cross, K. W. (1972), Psychiatric Day-Care in Birmingham. Brit. J. prev. soc. Med., 26, 112-120.
15. Cross, K. W., Hassall, Christine and Gath, D. (1972), Psychiatric Day-Care – the New Chronic Population. Brit. J. prev. soc. Med., 26, 199-204.
16. Hassall, Christine, The Worcester Development Project, Int. J. Ment. Health, Vol. 5, No. 3, 44-50.
17. Department of Health and Social Security (1970), *Feasibility Study for a model reorganisation of mental illness services.* London, H.M.S.O.
18. Baldwin, J. A. (1971), *The Mental Hospital in the Psychiatric Service.* London, Oxford University Press for the Nuffield Provincial Hospitals Trust.
19. Wing, J. K. (1971), Planning services for the mentally ill in Camberwell, in *Evaluating a Community Mental Health Service, ed.* Wing, J. K. and Hailey, A. M., London, Oxford University Press for the Nuffield Provincial Hospitals Trust.
20. Hailey, A. M. (1974), The New Chronic Psychiatric Population, Brit. J. prev. soc. Med. *28,* 180-186.
21. British Medical Journal Leading Article, (1976), Asylums are still needed. *Vol. 1,* 111-112.
22. Christie Brown, J. R. W., Ebringer, Lorna, and Freedman, L. S. (1977), A survey of a long-stay psychiatric population, Psychological Medicine, *7,* 113-126.

PART SIX

BOARDING OUT

7: Boarding-Out and Substitute Family Care of the Psychiatric Patient

M. Rolf Olsen

Papers 8 and 9 of this volume examine the use of boarding-out and family care in the rehabilitation of the chronic psychiatric patient. I have shown elsewhere[1,2] that in psychiatric care the terms 'Family Care' and 'Boarding-Out' although not really synonymous, in that the first implies foster or substitute family care and the second a physical or economic arrangement, are used to describe a system of care in which discharged psychiatric and mentally handicapped patients are cared for in non-institutional living groups which are not their own. Under this arrangement patients may be placed with families or in similar residences such as boarding-houses, either singly, in small groups, or in quite large groups of thirty or more.

The first recorded system of family care was in Gheel, Belgium, where it has been continually practised since the seventh-century. However, in spite of its long history and its successful adoption in a number of other European countries, it has not, since the nineteenth-century revelations which publicised the wretched condition of many lunatics living in private houses, been favoured in English or Welsh psychiatry.

Wing (1957)[3], during his review of family care systems in Norway and Holland, found that in England and Wales there were some 3,000 mental defectives in the community under the Guardianship scheme, many in foster homes. He also discovered that, although the system was acknowledged to work well, in spite of the provision for boarding-out certified patients under Section 57 of the Lunacy Act:—

"only 50-60 psychiatric patients are boarded out under it and it is clear that neither the Local Authorities nor the Hospital Management Committees are in favour of using it."

This situation compared unfavourably with Norway and Holland where Wing met a keen interest.

In Norway he found that 51 per cent of the certified were cared for in mental hospitals, 39 per cent were looked after in families and 10 per cent were in nursing homes. Wing felt that the percentage in family care was excessive and that many of the patients should have been hospitalised. He thought that

133

there was a shortage of hospital beds, particularly in remote areas, and that families were often being used as a substitute for hospital care and in consequence the system was under too much pressure to work ideally. Even so, the scheme commended itself. At the best organised centre, at Lier, it was estimated that 300 patients were boarded out from the hospital. These remained on the hospital register and patients were able to move in and out of the centre without repeat documentation. They were distributed in twos and threes, usually to crofters who were encouraged to treat the patient like a member of the family. Many other patients were boarded out by the local health authorities, and it was estimated that in the Lier Valley more than 1,000 psychotic and defective patients were boarded out in a total population of 14,000. It was rare for complaints to be made about the patient's behaviour, and no one seemed to think the arrangement had a bad effect on the children. The crime rate amongst the patient population was lower than the general population.

Wing emphasised that the organization at Lier was thorough, and that this was necessary to enable the system to work and to prevent exploitation of the patient. He felt that there was much for British psychiatry to learn from it.

In Holland, Wing found that many hospitals had some provision for family care. In Beilen a colony system has existed since 1922, when, as an experiment, 8 women were successfully placed in different families. There were few difficulties and the system grew so that by 1957 there were 370 patients, of whom about a third were defective, cared for in private homes. The colony was supported by a centre which took up to 100 in-patients, and which provided a wide variety of work and occupational therapy for the boarded out patients, almost all of whom attended the centre each day. None of the foster families lived more than one mile from the centre, and each was closely supported by the hospital personnel. High standards of care were laid down. No family was allowed to take more than three patients and each patient had his own room. Clothes, bedding and furniture were provided by the centre.

Wing conveyed the strengths of these different care systems and stressed particularly the humanity and personal liberty they afforded. Their basic weakness was seen to lie in the custodial attitude and the dependence that they created – it is rarely used as a short term measure. Wing concluded that:—

"after social and somatic treatment with a mental hospital, and with the support of other social services, there seems no reason to doubt that family care could contribute considerably towards the rehabilitation of many kinds of psychiatric patients".

Whilst boarding-out has not, until recently, been a favoured strategy in England and Wales, there has been a system of boarding-out in Scotland for well over 100 years. The basis for this practice is "to provide family care" with the intention "that the boarded-out person should be absorbed into the life of the guardian's home, and, as far as possible, into the life of the community" (1970)[4]. The system arose out of the 1845 Poor Law Act, when paupers became chargeable to the Parish, and those who were insane had to be lodged in an asylum or legally authorised institution; because little accommodation was available in the institutions, private houses were licensed. This is similar to the situation in North Wales today when, in the absence of Local Authority accommodation, the hospital has looked to private houses for an outlet.

In America the boarding-out system was introduced on a small scale in 1885 (Wing (1957)[3]), but it was not to gain ground until after the Second World War.

Muncie (1945)[5], in "a note on a practitioner's improvisation", reports in detail on 3 patients successfully placed in foster care. He gives no references in his paper, and claimed that at that time "foster home care for adults has received little if any attention in the literature", and relates that he stumbled on the idea in a "somewhat accidental fashion" after his realization of its usefulness in the care of children.

Throughout his paper Muncie stressed the naturalness of the procedure – "the complete antithesis of the hospital atmosphere" – and in all three cases he felt that the "foster home performed a service which could not be matched by hospital and could not have been obtained under any circumstances in the home environment".

Barton (1953)[6], in a review of the psychiatric progress in America during 1953, reported that "the slow growth in family care continues". He estimated that the total number boarded-out in his country had risen from 4,937 in 1951, to 5,617 in 1952, to 6,201 in 1953.

More recent papers, Friedman et al. (1966)[7], Fairweather et al. (1969)[8], Lamb et al. (1971)[9], Keskiner et al. (1972)[10], Chien et al. (1973)[11], and Sandall et al. (1975)[12], from America, show that in recent years "there has been a mass exodus of long-term mental patients from State hospitals" (Lamb et al.): that the "major thrust in hospital treatment programs during the past two decades has been to release chronic patients to protective community settings" (Keskiner et al.), and that the conclusion shared by many psychiatrists is that "many hospitalized psychotic patients can live and function in the community if a suitable sheltered environment is provided" (Chien et al.).

In England and Wales the major drive for the development of boarding-out care of the discharged psychiatric patient followed the Mental Health Act, 1959[13], and the 1962 Hospital Plan for England and Wales[14], both of which advocated that a greater share of the management of long-stay patients should be transferred back to the community. In the absence of alternative community-based accommodation, those psychiatric hospitals and local authorities who wished to implement the proposal had little option but to improvise and tap into existing community resources.

However, the use of boarding-house care had a slow start, "according to the Ministry of Health, 47 mentally ill patients were boarded-out in 1964; this figure had risen to 76 by the end of last year" (1967) Gregory.[15] These estimates, although rightly conveying the overall picture, are grossly inaccurate in that a number of institutions were by this time boarding-out. For example by the end of 1967 the North Wales Hospital Denbigh had itself placed 174 patients in boarding houses. In a written reply to me, 30.4.70, the Department of Health and Social Security stated, "we have no statistical information concerning patients boarded-out on discharge from psychiatric hospitals" (1970)[16].

In the absence of any central monitoring it is difficult to estimate the developments in boarding-out with accuracy. However, from 1959 several reports indicated that an increasing number of hospitals and authorities were employing this strategy to rehabilitate and discharge psychiatric patients, including the County Borough of Brighton (1959)[17], Somerset County Council (1960)[18], Severall's Hospital (1963)[19], Borough of Croydon (1962)[20], Exe Vale Psychiatric Hospital (1962)[21], and the Old Manor Hospital, Salisbury (1974)[22].

Boarding-Out: Circumventing and interrupting Chronicity or Relocalising the Miniature Institutions

The fundamental questions in relation to boarding-out are whether it is an effective and viable strategy in circumventing and/or interrupting chronicity, or whether it represents no more than a relocalising of psychiatric patients in miniature institutions.

The opinion in the quoted studies, apart from some minor reservations, suggests that boarding-out is not only a viable strategy but that it also offers the long-stay patient a number of advantages which would be denied if he remained in institutional care. In particular: the opportunity to return to and be supported by the community, personal family-based care, employment, increased privacy, greater self-determination, a greater dignity from the opportunity to contribute to their own and the well-being of others as opposed to the passive acceptance of institutional care, and avoidance of the worst features of institutional neurosis.

The hospital and the wider community are also felt to gain from the alleged financial savings and the better use of scarce hospital resources.

There are, however, a number of authors who reject these conclusions and argue that, whilst it is true that hospital populations and the length of hospitalisation have been reduced, in some institutions the patients have not achieved the benefits outlined above. Some argue that circumventing a long-stay in hospital is artificial in that, whilst it reduced the length of stay, it has resulted in a new disguised chronicity referred to as "intermittent patienthood" (Friedman et al.[7]). This status and condition is characterised by repeated admission to hospital which leads to an institutional dependency and loss of family ties in much the same way as occurs in the single, long admission.

Others, Fairweather et. al.[8] and Lamb et. al.[9], argue that, whilst boarding houses have enabled the long-stay patient to be discharged, they have a low expectation of achievement, docility is valued, and little initiative is expected. In consequence, "the boarding-house group is not really in the community. It is like a small ward moved to a community setting" (Lamb et. al.[9]).

Darley and Kenny[23], during their investigation of the low success rate of a day centre for psychiatric patients, came to the same conclusion that discharge often represents no more than a relocation of the patient in a different institutional setting, or sheltered sub-society in which the patient is "given the damaging role of citizen-on-probation".

Keskiner et. al.[10] also dismiss the alleged benefits of boarding-out care arrangements, arguing that:

"1. Chronic patients lack the social and vocational skills necessary for functioning independently in the community;

2. mental health manpower and financial resources are being utilised to maintain them in miniature institutions; and

3. the community is not providing the acceptance or the assistance essential for the social reintegration."

The authors, however, do not reject the principles of community care, rather they argue that if we are successfully to apply them we must construct a re-socialisation programme which is designed not only to prepare the patient for community living but also the whole "foster community" – on the lines of Gheel – to adopt "psychiatric patients as new citizens".

Chien et. al.[11] claim that boarding-out and similar arrangements such as half-way houses, hostels, nursing homes and independent living all have serious limitations. They argue that half-way houses and hostels are difficult to establish and expensive to run, family care promotes dependency, nursing care contains the worst features of institutional living, and independent living isolates the patient from essential contact.

They conclude, as do others (Sandall et. al.[12]), that landlord-supervised co-operative apartments, a hybrid of foster family care and independent living, which provides a semi-independent living in low-rent accommodation, are financially and logistically superior to other arrangements in that the patient can enjoy the support of a neighbour/landlord or non-psychiatric tenant yet maintain some privacy and independence.

Whilst the contradictory conclusions contained within the quoted papers point to some of the fundamental problems of family care and boarding-out, none reject the feasibility of placing chronic patients in non-institutional living groups, or invalidate the concept in any way. Rather they argue for alternative systems within the overall policy to return long-stay patients to the community and raise the major issues which arise out of the strategy.

The next two papers relate the outcome of two boarding-out schemes and show that with important reservations substitute family care can be very successful and offer a viable alternative which has many advantages over hospital care.

References

1. Olsen, M. R. (1976), Boarding-Out the Long-Stay Psychiatric Patient, in *Differential Approaches in Social Work with the Mentally Disordered,* BASW.
2. Olsen, M. R. (1976), *The Personal and Social Consequences of the Discharge of the Long-stay Psychiatric Patient from the North Wales Hospital, Denbigh (1965-66),* Ph.D. Thesis, Univ. of Wales.
3. Wing, J. K. (1957), Family Care Systems in Norway and Holland, *Lancet,* Vol. 2, 884-886.
4. Mental Welfare Commission for Scotland (1970), *Boarding Out in Scotland.*
5. Muncie, W. (1945), Foster Home for Adults, *J. Ment. Dis.* Vol. 102, 477-482.
6. Barton, W. E. (1953), Out-Patient Psychiatry and Family Care, *Am. J. Psychiat.,* Vol. 110, pp. 533.
7. Friedman, I., Von Mering, O. and Hinko, E. N. (1966), Intermittent Patienthood, *Arch. Gen. Psychiat.,* 14: 386-392.

8. Fairweather, G. W., Sanders, D. H., Maynard, H. (1969), *Community Life for the Mentally Ill: An Alternative to Institutional Care,* Chicago, Aldine.

9. Lamb, H. R. and Goertzel, V. (1971), Discharged Mental Patients—Are they really in the Community?, *Arch. Gen. Psychiat.,* 24: 29-34.

10. Keskiner, A., Zalman, M. J., Ruppert, E. H. and Ulett, G. A. (1972), The Foster Community: A Partnership in Psychiatric Rehabilitation, *Am. J. Psychiat.,* 129:3, Sept. 1972, 283-288.

11. Chien, C. P. and Cole, J. O. (1973), Landlord-Supervised Co-operative Apartments: A New Modality for Community Based Treatment, *Am. J. Psychiat.,* 130:2, Feb. 1973, 156-169.

12. Sandall, H., Hawley, T. T. and Gordon, G. C. (1975), The St. Louis Community Homes Program: Graduated Support for Long-Term Care, *Am. J. Psychiat.,* June 1975, 132-136.

13. *Mental Health Act,* 1959, H.M.S.O., London.

14. Ministry of Health (1962), *The Hospital Plan for England and Wales,* H.M.S.O., Cmnd. 1904.

15. Gregory, E. (1968), Landladies for the Mentally Ill, *New Society* 324, 879-880.

16. D.H.S.S., Letter 30.4.70.

17. Chief Mental Health Officer, County Borough of Brighton, Letter 1.6.70.

18. Parry-Jones, A., Buchan, A. R. and Beasley, J., Ten Years of Boarding-Out in Somerset, *Lancet,* 3.10.70, 712-714.

19. Whitehead, J. A., A Comprehensive Psycho-Geriatric Service, *Lancet,* 18.9.65, 583-586.

20. Heap, J. S., Principal Mental Health Officer, Croydon, Letter 21.5.70.

21. Slater, H., Community Care for the Mentally Frail, *Social Work Today,* 17.6.71, Vol. 2, No. 6, 3-8.

22. Smith, C., Institutional Dependence is Reversible, *Social Work Today,* 16.10.75, Vol. 6, No. 14, 426-428.

23. Darley, P. J. and Kenny, W. J. (1971), Community Care and the "Queequeg Syndrome" – a Phenomenological Evaluation of Methods of Rehabilitation for Psychotic Patients, *Amer. J. Psychiat.,* 127: 1333-1338.

8: Family Substitute Care in the Rehabilitation of the Discharged Psychiatric Patient
Gertrude Smith

Summary

A previous article entitled "Institutional Dependence is Reversible[1] (1975) described a scheme whereby a number of long-stay patients were discharged from a small psychiatric hospital in Salisbury to supported lodgings provided by landladies who had agreed to accept these patients as residents in the family home. The initial number of places was 100 but since then another 30 have been similarly placed. Of the original long-stay patients remaining in hospital very few are considered suitable to leave the institution.

Taken as a whole, the scheme was successful. However, there are certain aspects, described in this article, which on appraisal suggest the approaches which might be adopted in future schemes.

Introduction

A number of schemes have been successfully established for patients to live in the community who have been dependent on living in an institution. Oxford, Somerset, Colchester and several others come within this category. Many psychiatric hospitals have halved the number of beds occupied by careful choice of patients who could live in the community; in a group home, half-way house, warden supervised bungalow, residential home for instance. Some of these were sponsored by local authorities, voluntary organisations or private landlords.

The following account is of a project undertaken by a group at the Old Manor Hospital, Salisbury, whereby some 97 long-stay patients have been discharged to private homes to become a member of a 'family' to whom they were not related and 37 to nursing home care. In two cases, two or more patients went together because they had become friends in the hospital and did not wish to be separated. The project is a descriptive account intended to convey what can be achieved with minimal expense.

Once we had decided to discharge long term patients the number of patients who were considered suitable for discharge grew daily, but the number of available beds in local authority residential homes was so limited that some scheme had to be devised if the beds in hospital were to be available for short-term treatable patients. The majority of those not actually receiving psychiatric treatment were over sixty years of age, some over seventy years and the oldest 88 years. None of these were considered able to look after themselves in supervised flats or group homes because they needed all the services normally provided for the elderly in their homes.

Although some areas have psychogeriatric assessment units, this hospital is not so fortunate. In any case when assessed, many patients would have nowhere to go unless their families were able to have them home after treatment.

Age Range

Table 1 shows that all but 15 were aged over 60 on discharge and that 18 per cent were aged 80 or over.

Table 1

Age Range on Discharge

Ages	Numbers	%
Over 40	1	.76
Over 50	14	10.76
Over 60	61	46.92
Over 70	31	23.84
Over 80	23	17.69
Total	130	100

The task

The team consisted of a psychiatrist (a number of consultants participated according to the ward concerned) a member of the nursing administration and rehabilitation staff, an occupational therapist, a member of the domicilary nursing staff and a social worker. The early meetings were concerned with discussing the scheme in principle; we needed to identify the main areas where difficulties would arise. A change of attitude by the whole hospital staff was essential if we were to encourage patients to move. It was soon established that dependence on the institution is not the sole prerogative of the patient! We encountered resistance among all levels of staff; perhaps a healthy initiation into the problems to come. No-one enjoys change and the notion of moving patients, after so many years of security in hospital, conjured up feelings of apprehension and fear and a foreboding that disasters would result in blame falling on the hospital and the staff. There were fantasies of court cases, newspaper reports and complaints by members of the public.

For some years past, one or two of the psychiatric nurses had been taking patients for holidays and into their own homes, so as a start, we built this up and asked others known to us to consider patients with whom they were acquainted. It seemed wise to ensure that all the first patients who left stood a very good chance of settling down as this would encourage others to offer their services and open their homes.

One patient who had no active psychiatric treatment for 15 years, owned a house she had let for £1 a week to a tenant who refused to vacate the premises. She was helped to go to court to claim her house in preparation for her discharge. The Recorder was so sympathetic that he immediately made an order giving her possession in three months; he also posed an awkward question 'Can you tell me why you waited 15 years before taking this step?'.

Gradually, the group became enthusiastic, especially when the first patient agreed to 'see how I get on'. As a preparation, the rehabilitation team had taken groups of patients for holidays to hotels at the seaside, some went camping and simultaneously the occupational therapy staff undertook to create a new climate of independence for individual patients in respect of caring for their clothes, stimulating interests, learning new and sometimes long-forgotten skills. In many cases, the physiotherapist assisted in helping patients to be more mobile, to mount stairs or to get into the bath. All felt encouraged by the genuine friendly attitude shown by members in the community.

Method

A consultant psychiatrist and a social worker interviewed individually every patient in the long-stay wards and with the charge nurse decided whether they could live outside the hospital provided that the environment appeared appropriate. Most of the patients were pleased to discuss their feelings, their physical state, the work they were doing, the entertainments provided, and their present accommodation. Quite casually, we mentioned the idea of leaving the hospital if the right place could be found. And the answer was prompt and predictable; 'It's very kind of you, doctor, I am sure, but I am happy here and would prefer to stay'. Some were reflective and non-commital, but later returned to say 'I'd rather not go, thank you all the same, Dr. So and So promised me I could stay for the rest of my life'.

The interviews were repeated at intervals because word went round the wards that patients would be sent out and anxiety was rising. 'Mrs. A is leaving next week, who will be the next?' One need hardly mention here that no one at all was moved unless they had consented and been consulted as to where they wanted to go.

At the same time as these interviews took place, negotiations were started with next-of-kin and relatives some of whom were helpful and very concerned for the patient's welfare. But others were angry and some openly hostile. As this hospital had before 1954 been a Licensed House, some patients had private means, the extent of which was known only to the relatives or to the Court of Protection and, where there was no Receiver, to the Official Solicitor. It became abundantly clear that the relatives who were reluctant concerning the discharge had two major fears: first that they would be responsible if the patient broke down and secondly that they might have to bear the financial burden themselves. When given reassurance on these issues, attitudes changed and we then enjoyed helpful collaboration and assistance. The ones who needed more nursing and had substantial means, were found places reasonably quickly in nursing homes or rest homes but these were only a relatively small number since the cost was usually £40-£60 per week and over.

Finding accommodation

The nursing staff not only volunteered themselves, but also encouraged some of their friends and relatives to participate. An advertisement in the local newspaper produced a few addresses though most of these were more suitable for those patients who were working and living in the local authority hostel until they were ready for total discharge. We used every available contact and visited each landlady to tell her about the scheme, the safeguards and the financial situation.

With hindsight, I wonder whether landladies were given a sufficiently full and frank explanation about what it means to have someone living in one's house as a member of the family. Although the relapse rate has been small (8.6%) one cannot overlook the fact that the residents have spent a great deal of time in hospital and indicate that they are often still dependent upon the

144

hospital staff and routine. The small failure rate suggests that the placements were appropriate. This view is confirmed by the residents who, when asked, say they would not like to return to the hospital and expressed themselves quite strongly that they were happy where they were and wished they had considered leaving hospital much earlier.

Financial Aspects

In any discharge scheme the questions relating to financing the patient undoubtedly cause the largest single headache. We frequently had to wait several weeks before the financial responsibility for the patient could be established, particularly when it involved the Court of Protection and the Pensions Board.

For the majority Social Security pays the major proportion (£22.35) for the supported lodgings, currently priced at £24 per week. Local Authorities pay the balance of £1.65, under the permissive powers contained in the Health Service and Public Health Act 1968, section 12. The resident receives £4.70 per week if under pensionable age and £5.25 per week if over this age, for personal spending. Because the Old Manor Hospital was a private hospital which received patients from anywhere in England before the formation of the Health Service, many of the Local Authorities from whence they came had no knowledge of the patients and were therefore very reluctant to meet any costs. Also many of the boundaries had been changed since the patient's admission and this created additional problems when trying to collect money for the particular individual. In some cases we approached Charitable Trusts and Ex-Service Pensions Boards who were extremely helpful. However, in spite of these difficulties no patient was prevented from doing so because the money was not available. In the case of the Court of Protection we found reluctance to resort to the use of capital even when the patients had achieved the age of 75 or over.

Where residents had private means, Nursing Homes and Rest Homes were found (the cost in these was generally between £60 and £70 a week).

Aftercare

It appears to be expedient to arrange an initial period with a review after approximately two or three weeks. This idea provides security both for the patient and the landlady and gives an opportunity to assess the adaptation to the new life and the break with the past.

The type of after-care or follow-up is undoubtedly the most important aspect of the whole project because, here again, there can be no single answer to meet the essential need of the individual. The decision is usually taken by the consultant psychiatrist with the patient and any other person or persons who may be involved. We have a variety of services, both voluntary and statutory. Sometimes, the patient has started by coming to the day hospital five days a week, transport provided by the hospital car service. This has been tapered off as soon as possible. Others attend industrial or occupational therapy at the hospital, one continues to work in the library, one has sole charge of the aviary. Some have been introduced to outside luncheon clubs, Women's Institutes and church groups. Social workers in the area, as well as those based in the hospital, may visit; and neighbours, relatives and friends all contribute to enrich the life of the person who is embarking on the fresh start. One could say that the most vital single service which has ensured the success of the venture has been and is the regular visits of the psychiatric nurse whose function is to co-ordinate many of the services and also to give, where appropriate, the maintenance injections. The skill and also the particular relationship of the nurse to the former patient provides support not available through other sources.

A particularly pleasing aspect has been that one has seen the degree of involvement that the landladies have been ready to share. Their guests have been invited to visit other members of the family, their friends, share in anniversary celebrations and go with them on holidays both in this country and abroad. One lady, who had been in hospital over thirty years enjoyed a holiday in Ireland with the family she now looks upon as her own. Most of them now talk of 'we' and 'my family' and really feel they belong to the family group. The women are encouraged to help in the house, with the shopping and the children, the men with the garden, the car and household repairs. One or two are attending classes at the local technical college or evening sessions. Two have joined the music society, one sings in the choir, the other plays in the local orchestra.

It has not been found necessary to provide an after-care service for those patients discharged to nursing homes. We have found that these residents settled very well in their new surroundings, made friends with other residents, were able to use the lounges and dining rooms freely and generally seemed to make a home and be assimilated more readily into community life. The matrons who ran these establishments have been particularly anxious to rehabilitate their residents and have arranged outings, occupations and entertainments which have been quite different to those provided in hospital.

Re-admission

Whilst re-admission to hospital cannot be held as a totally reliable indication of the success or failure of the scheme it does provide information about the number who were unable to remain in the community. Table 2 shows that overall 7.7 per cent returned to hospital. The primary complaint which led to the patient's re-admission were, incontinence, quarrelsome, garrulous, and wandering into other people's rooms and helping themselves to their possessions.

Table 2

Readmission to Hospital

Accommodation	No. Discharged	No. Readmitted	%
Supported Lodgings	93	8	8.6
Nursing Homes	37	2	5.4
TOTAL	130	10	7.7

Conclusions

To date 130 long-stay, mostly elderly patients have been discharged under this scheme. The findings suggest that it has been successful and supports the conclusions of my earlier paper[1], firstly, that institutional dependence is reversible; secondly, that supported lodgings are a viable strategy, and thirdly that they may be preferable to residential and group homes for the elderly person who is unable to meet the level of achievements which they demand.

The findings also confirm that such schemes need to pay attention to a number of issues, not only to ensure successful rehabilitation, but also to prevent chronicity and long stays in hospital. In particular the needs and anxieties of relatives must be understood and met if we are to prevent the weakening and severence of family ties during long hospitalisation and we must seek ways to ensure that the patient maintains links and contact with the community; the preparation for discharge must include opportunity to learn the skills which will be required; it is essential to involve volunteers and the community not only in discharge but in the life of the hospital to ensure that the bridges with the community are maintained, and a consultant psychiatrist and senior social worker should be appointed to each institution with special responsibility for rehabilitation. Once discharge has been effected patients, landladies and volunteers must have ready access to professional advice and support. Lastly we must ensure that supported lodgings are not always seen as the final solution and that regular consideration is given to moving the patient to greater independence.

Reference

1. Smith, G. (1975), Institutional Dependence is Reversible, *Social Work Today,* Vol. 6, No. 14, pp. 426-28.

9: Community Care for the Mentally Frail

Helen Slater

Summary

In 1962 a survey carried out by the senior medical and nursing staff of the Exe Vale Psychiatric Hospital, Exminster, indicated that of the 1,600 patients approximately half no longer required hospital care.

An experiment was started with the aim of the rehabilitation of this group in the community and during the 15 years under review over 2,000 patients have been discharged to carefully selected private accommodation. Less than 8% return to remain in hospital. Table 1 indicates the extent to which the scheme is contributing in helping patients to return to the community, and Table 2 the effect on the size of the hospital population.

Table 1

Number of patients discharged to private Registered Accommodation

Year	1962	1963	1964	1969	1970	1974
Number	33(1)	31(1)	122(1)	118(1)(2)	189(1)(3)	163

(1) all females   (2) 21% of all discharges   (3) 33% of all discharges

Table 2

Total hospital population 1960 – 1977

1960	1,600
1970	1,000
1977	700

A survey (see Appendix 1) covering five homes shows that re-admissions can also be significantly reduced. Of twenty-six patients with a total record of sixty-five admissions, only one of this group has required re-admission since being discharged to an environment selected to meet individual needs. The

149

efforts of the social worker have been directed to finding a *home* for the patient, not a substitute hospital or hostel.

Whilst the experiment was started to help the long-stay patient, priority is now given to new admissions who, when ready for discharge, cannot return for medical/social reasons to their admission address. During 1970 of the 189 female patients discharged to selected accommodation, 92 had been in hospital less than nine weeks, 19 had been in over thirty years! Since 1964 all admissions have been in the over sixty age group.

The implications of the scheme are:—

(1) In the main patients can leave hospital without delay when they are ready to be discharged to an environment selected to meet their needs.

(2) Hospital beds and nursing and medical skills can be more fully used for those who need hospital care and long waiting lists for admissions are avoided.

(3) It involves the community in 'caring'.

(4) The financial savings are considerable.

(5) The development of the scheme has resulted in the social worker always knowing of at least ten vacancies.

Introduction

The Hospital and the Experiment

The Exminster section of the Exe Vale Hospital group in 1960 was faced with the same problem as many other hospitals – of the 1,600 patients half this number no longer required hospital care, they remained there simply because they had no home to go to and no one to care for them. The social services had not responded to the needs created by the achievements of the medical profession and the provisions of the Mental Health Act 1959 and other post-war legislation.

An experiment was started to help these patients into the community and was based on experience gained in Exeter (1954-60) when the Council of Social Service and Old People's Welfare Committee developed a boarding out scheme for the elderly with financial help from the National Corporation for the Care of Old People and later from the City Council. That scheme had begun very slowly, there was so much to learn but it developed in scope and scale and a local psychiatric hospital sought our help, as did other agencies. We were pleasantly surprised to find a number of those who had offered a

150

home were willing to consider having patients who had been in hospital many years. It was thought with the development of the scheme the trend would be for the private homes to cater for those who presented fewer problems and the local authorities making provision for those with greater needs. Twenty-four years later the position is the reverse. In the main local authority homes are not geared to helping the mentally frail and the private homes in the areas where the scheme has been developed are making a substantial contribution to meeting this need.

The experience with the Council of Social Service convinced me the community could make a worthwhile contribution to the problem of accommodation and care for the elderly and the mentally frail. When I left in 1960 three of the staff were involved in this work and, had any of them joined the hospital staff as I did, it would be reasonable to assume that the results would have been similar.

In the early years when I was with the Exeter Council of Social Services I addressed many Annual Conferences in different parts of the country. Invariably the audiences were sharply divided either for or against the scheme. One side almost claiming that it was answer to the problem of accommodation and care for the elderly and those against showing a great reluctance to accept that the scheme had a contribution to make in meeting a social need.

Broadly speaking members of the medical profession felt that the scheme could be very helpful and wished to see it developed in other parts of the country. This attitude also applied locally where The Medical Officer of Health took a keen interest in the progress of the scheme and contributed to a medical journal on the subject.

The opinion of the local Welfare Officer is perhaps best described by his comment to me "I wouldn't touch it with a barge pole". Over the years I have linked this kind of Local Authority attitude with the reaction of relatives who are unable or unwilling to care for a patient but feel that they ought to do so.

At one conference I attended a Welfare officer held up his hands in horror when we met. Some time previous he had read about the scheme, had found a number of homes and *"placed"* twenty-seven elderly people. In a very short time he had them all back. Better to have a barge pole attitude.

Opinions about whether a patient needs to remain in hospital varies a good deal and to a large extent it depends on the quality and level of care in the community. The difference in medical opinion has been very clearly brought out since the Team system has been introduced into Exe Vale Hospital in

1971. It comes to notice when a patient is transferred from an admission ward to a long-stay ward which is under the care of a different Consultant. Many patients in this group have been discharged. They have been absorbed into the general picture of patients discharged and have not presented any distinguishing features.

In my opinion this situation, e.g. when patients are transferred to long-stay wards, arises when the medical staff have not had the opportunity of assessing, or indeed are not aware of the kind of care which is available outside hospital. It is possible that some have assumed that because the patient was not acceptable in L.A. Part III accommodation that there was no alternative to hospitalisation. The majority of the 2,000 patients discharged to private Registered Homes would in fact have been considered unsuitable by the Local Authority for Part III. From time to time a resident in Part III is transferred direct to a private Registered Home. This is arranged when a resident needs more care or a different kind of care than Part III can provide. It is done in the interest of the resident who may well be feeling rejected, and of The Home which may not be geared to meeting the particular needs.

Table 3

Length of Stay in Hospital before discharge to Registered Private Homes

Length of stay	1962 — 1964		1969		1970		1974
	Number	%	Number	%	Number	%	Number
Up to 6 months	0	0	90	76	129*	68	Dates of
7 — 11 months	0	0	1	1	10	5	admission
1 yr — 10 yrs	119	49	8	7	15	8	and
11 yrs — 20 yrs	87	35	2	2	7	4	discharge
21 yrs — 30 yrs	30	12	8	6	10	5	not
31 yrs — 40 yrs	8	3	6	5	9	5	readily
41 yrs — 50 yrs	2	1	2	2	9	5	available
51 yrs — 55 yrs	0	0	1	1	0	0	
Totals	246	100	118	100	189	100	163

* 92 of these were in hospital 2 to 8 weeks.

N.B. No accurate figures are readily available for the years 1965, 1966, 1967 and 1968. The average was probably 120 per year and it can be assumed that since 1961, more than 2,000 patients who had no home to return to have been found suitable accommodation in the community and discharged.

There was some initial resistance to the experiment from several directions – patients, relatives who preferred the patient to remain in hospital, sometimes for financial reasons, some nursing staff – one charge nurse said "you'll be working me out of a bloody job!" Some ward sisters who had cared for the same patients for many years were, perhaps naturally, apprehensive and unhappy about them leaving hospital. One, now retired, was always resistant and I was therefore surprised one day when she asked me if I could find a home for a patient. During the course of the conversation she mentioned that she was "the most difficult patient on the ward". Many of the patients no longer needing hospital care were good workers and gave considerable help in running the hospital. I was asked "How can I run my hospital if you take all my best workers?" The National Assistance Board Officers were not always helpful and a crisis situation arose when they refused to pay more than £3.10s per week for six patients who had settled in the community. Regional and Head Office were involved and after much discussion and further consideration the allowance was brought up to the required amount of £4.10s. I confess to having a pretty rough ride during the first year or two!

The breaking of relationships in a closed institution brings many heartaches and separation conflicts, even though the relationship is on a staff/patient basis. Additionally, a society which for centuries had incarcerated its mentally ill members, suddenly though painfully was re-adjusting to an acceptance that mental illness could be coped with by means other than in major institutions. Change brings stress and it is not surprising that in this situation initial resistance was strong.

Table 4
Age Distribution of patients discharged to selected
Registered Private Homes

Age Range	1962-1963-1964		1969		1970		1971 – 1977
	Number	%	Number	%	Number	%	
Under 60	52	21	5	4	8	4	
60—69	71	29	32	27	59	31	
70—79	94	38	36	31	82	44	See*[2]
80—89	25	10	38	32	38	20	note
90+	4	2	7	6	2	1	below
Totals	246*[1]	100	118	100	189	100	163

*[1] 1962 = 33; 1963 = 91; 1964 = 122
*[2] Figures of age groups are not readily available for 1971 – 77 but it is known that there were few aged under 60 and that the majority were in the 75 – 85 age groups, i.e. very similar to previous years.

However, as one patient after another left the hospital and did not return the apprehension and resistance faded and interest and support increased. Patients themselves became involved and took the initiative in approaching the ward sister or social worker – some asked if they could join a friend who had left, one asked "are you the lady that gets people out?" Without the full support at medical level, which once confidence had been established, was given in full measure, the development of the scheme would have been impossible. Table 4 shows that age is no barrier to discharging the patient. The results indicate the contribution that the good registered home can make in reducing the number of re-admissions as well as the total number of patients.

Developments Since 1971

In 1971 the Consultants in the hospital grouped themselves into four area teams with nursing and social work staff. This review refers to my work with the South Team comprising three Consultants with 37 admission beds.

As a direct result of this re-organisation there had developed a strong team spirit between the nursing and medical staff and the social worker, giving each other and particularly the social worker, considerable support. Also, it has provided a valuable basis for the development of good and happy professional relationships.

The people running the Home now visit the hospital for a variety of reasons, i.e., to meet a possible new patient, to pick up a patient, to bring a former patient for review by the Consultant etc., and the team structure, with its unified policy, portrays the hospital in a way which is helpful. On these visits discussions take place with the nursing staff, not only on the particular reasons for the visit but on the progress of former patients. The smaller team has helped to establish better lines of communication and closer personal relationships both inside and outside the hospital, and eases arrangements when the social worker is on leave. Nursing staff have also visited the Homes and know the people running them making team discussions on discharge arrangements more interesting and meaningful.

Patients can be discharged and re-admitted with little delay. If a former patient in a Registered Home needs urgent re-admission this can usually be arranged quickly. Because of this and the medical and social worker support Homes are often able and willing to ride through a difficult patch and the need for re-admission is avoided. Without this kind of understanding they would probably feel unable to carry on.

Our wide knowledge of Registered Homes in the area has other benefits. For example, if a former patient's condition changes to the point where she needs more care or a different kind of Home for other reasons, but not re-admission, a transfer to an alternative Home can be arranged.

After the scheme started it was arranged for the social worker to have an office near to the wards and also adjoining the Team Consultants' Offices. This proved to be extremely helpful. Along with other advantages this simple re-arrangement enabled her to observe the patients more often in the ward setting – very essential in making a social assessment.

Before deciding whether to discharge a patient to a Home a social worker needs to know several things about the patient's behaviour. For example: Does the patient make friends, seek the company of a group, an individual, or prefer solitude? Does she join in any activities, read newspapers, watch T.V., show initiative in any way, get on with people and with what kind of people? Has she any strong likes or dislikes? Does she smoke and what is the level of fire risk? Does she go out, and how much? Does she prefer the country or going around the shops? Does she attend Church? Do any friends or relatives visit her and how does she respond to their visits? What is the going-to-bed and getting-up pattern? Are there any problems with diet? Have the patient's characteristics changed since admission and what have been the main factors in bringing about the change? Does she like to be known by her Christian name? etc.

The answers to many of these questions and others can be gained by observation, supplemented by informal and seemingly unplanned chats on the ward. Many patients cannot sustain a long discussion and these kind of meetings oil the wheels of communication and help to establish confidence. It leads to discussion on problems and future plans in an easy and natural way.

Additionally the new office arrangement enabled me to see more relatives and to have those informal chats with medical and nursing staff which make for good communications. In turn patients, relatives, nursing and medical staff were able to visit me in my office. Previously it was so far away from the wards that this rarely happened.

The increase in the level of State benefits has enabled those dependent on a supplementary pension or allowance (50% of the group under review) to make a reasonable payment for rent and have a margin for personal expenses. With the present level of charges in the Registered Homes, between £38-£45 per week, it is reasonable to expect good standards of care and comfortable living conditions. It is equally fair that the level of state allowances should continue to increase with the level of inflation.

The Attendance Allowance, which most of the patients qualify for, has been a tremendous help. The majority in this group need considerable care and attention and often frequent changes of personal clothing and of bedding are required. The additional income enables patients to meet the higher charges involved and the Homes are to employ additional staff and meet high laundry costs.

The development over the years of good relationships between the Homes and the Hospital has stimulated discussion in the community and has helped at grass roots level in the spread of knowledge, and the lessening of prejudice and misunderstanding.

As the Matrons gain in experience and confidence so they are able to understand and meet the needs of the patient, e.g., being aware of and sensitive to the patient's apprehension when leaving hospital and their initial feelings of loneliness in strange surroundings and with new faces all around. They have learnt the importance of allowing the patient to go at her own pace and settle in her own way and they know too of the need to reserve judgment. A move to new surroundings can have a disturbing effect and a new resident's behaviour is often very different after a week or two.

The acceptance by the South Team of the policy to make every effort to find suitable alternative accommodation for patients ready to be discharged, has resulted in the nursing and medical staff on the admission wards having the satisfaction of seeing their patients leave hospital. It is disheartening to them to have to transfer a patient who is ready to be discharged to what may not be a very suitable ward with a note "awaiting outside accommodation". We try to avoid the use of the words "long-stay ward". It can be distressing to the patient and is certainly bewildering to a relative to be told that a patient has been transferred to a long-stay ward and to be contacted perhaps only a few weeks later to discuss arrangements. The term "further observation ward" is more appropriate to the situation.

About the Patients

Patients with a wide range of disorders from the spectrum of social backgrounds continue to be helped by the scheme. The two largest diagnostic groups are those suffering from recurrent depression or senile dementia. The fact that the majority of those suffering from recurrent depression discharged to a carefully selected Home have not returned to hospital, suggests that the home situation was an important factor contributing to the cause of the condition, e.g., loneliness, family stress, inadequacy, lack of care and good food, not taking medication, etc. The case of patients suffering from marked senile dementia was a real challenge and the five Homes which care for residents with dementia with the maximum freedom compatible with safety and the reasonable comfort of others are run by people with considerable psychiatric nursing experience.

It is rewarding to see an elderly person who was admitted in a mood of frustration and unhappiness eventually settled in an enviornment which permits her to develop her own style of occupational therapy (which might be just walking around all day) and daily routine. It is extremely difficult to provide this kind of environment in a small family home. Some quietly spend time in their bedroom taking their clothes out of a drawer and putting them back again, others undertake knitting or stitching. Perhaps the most satisfying occupation is a simple domestic task like polishing a table or the brass. I have been surprised to see how well very confused patients can cope with once familiar tasks.

In endeavouring to create interest, however, it is essential to exercise judgment. There are some who are content just to sit and watch and have no desire to be active in any way and in my view their choice of this way of life should be respected.

Giving Up One's Home

When it first becomes apparent that a patient is unable to return to live alone it is very undesirable, in my view, that the question of the sale of the house or the termination of the tenancy is brought up at that stage unless the patient indicates a wish to discuss the matter. To put it to a patient that perhaps it is time she thought of giving up her home before she has any ideas about where she can go makes her unduly anxious and threatened.

The first essential step is to carefully explain to the patient the reasons why it would be inadvisable to return straight to her home from hospital and to discuss with her a possible alternative as a first step. At this stage the patient needs a considerable amount of support from the Team nursing staff and social worker and here the co-ordinated Team approach and good communications has proved of great help to the patients.

After leaving hospital, it is essential the patient is allowed time to adjust before the question of the disposal of the house is brought up. As far as possible, and within reason it should be left to the patient to indicate when she is able to face up to making a decision.

Giving up one's home is a major decision – there may be little or even no

157

choice for the person concerned but it is still painful. Relatives often need help in understanding these points, so that they can sensitively help the patient to make the right decision.

A considerable number of former patients have spent a year or more moving between a Registered Home and their own home, going home when they felt they were well enough (but very possibly were not) and returning to the Registered Home when they were ill, often preceded by an S.O.S. to the Registered Home from a relative, neighbour, or the patient herself. This "taking time" to make the final decision presents many administrative difficulties. Each move can involve change of address for D.H.S.S. order books, a change of post office and G.P., the next of kin may need to be informed and at short notice the Matron is called upon to do all these things, as well as welcoming the patient back.

The Homes are encouraged to enable residents to have some of their personal things with them such as a bedside table, a favourite chair, photographs and sometimes personal towels and bed linen. Occasionally a cat or dog has been included but this in my view is not to be recommended. The problems caused by, for instance, a chair which is too large for the available space is nothing when compared with the problems which can erupt when a cat or dog arrives on the scene.

The Homes

At the beginning of the experiment the need for a sound assessment by the Matron was fully recognised and after fifteen years experience it is still regarded as the first essential step. There is no substitute for this, neither inspection visits nor regulations will protect residents if the people running the Home are not of good character or lack the qualities needed for this kind of work.

The scheme developed gradually and in several ways. Those who had patients talked to their friends and relatives about their "work with the hospital" and new offers of homes were received. The whole scheme has, over the years been built on good personal relationships between the Hospital, general practitioners, Department of Health and Social Security, the people providing the homes and the patients. The present position is that the South Team has a list of 34 homes providing over 800 beds where they are happy to take patients from hospital.

Some of the homes are on main roads, others are in residential or country areas. Standards vary a good deal and include Homes very attractively furnished with fitted carpets and pleasing floral arrangements, while some have a well used look and a distinct family atmosphere.

Twelve of the people who first took patients have bought a larger house or extended the existing one. Three Homes where they now have 40 patients between them were referred to the social worker by consultants who, on making a domiciliary visit noted the caring qualities of the Home and a potential interest in people with mental health problems.

It was quickly evident that some long-stay patients while responding to a homely atmosphere found difficulty in adjusting to being in a small home with just one or two other people. This fact has contributed to the development of larger Homes.

Once in the community and away from the unnatural environment of hospital there are more opportunities for the patient to pursue personal interests. Shops, clubs, churches, cinemas etc., friends and relatives are sometimes nearer and many patients have responded to the more personal and homely environment to an extent which has been surprising.

The People Running the Homes and What This Involves

For convenience I have referred to patients as 'she', but the scheme provides help to men and women alike. Also in referring to the key person running the Home, I have used the title Matron. This is unsuitable as it gives the wrong image; it is not used by the residents and I would prefer not to either, but it is linguistically convenient.

Their ages range from 21 to 70+ and include widows and married couples, fifteen of whom have young children at home. Some have nursing, including psychiatric qualifications, and all have the quality of caring for people as individuals and can appreciate emotional as well as material needs. They come from varied home backgrounds, differ greatly in personal appearance and include Irish, Indian, Italian, German, Polish as well as those from different counties in this country, each bringing an individual contribution to the whole scheme. Some are excellent for those who need and respond to 'mothering' – they can demonstrate affection in a natural and sincere way. Several have the special skill required to help those who have lost their confidence – perhaps because of the nature of their illness or a long period in hospital – and can judge the timing and pace, and this is very important, at which a patient can take a further step into community life. Some can be firm as well as kind! Others have the knack of providing the kind of environment where personalities can find expression. Several have experience of mental illness within their own family circle, and a number have fostered or adopted children, others have taken in an unmarried mother and her child; the quality of caring shows itself in many ways. For the very frail of course homes are needed where a high standard of physical care, kindness and supervision is available.

The qualities we look for include integrity, kindness, common-sense, ability to cope with crises, supported by a fundamental respect for the individual. A sense of humour is helpful! An expectation of high standards of 'caring' is implicit in the scheme. Many of the staff are relatives or friends, which adds to the family-like atmosphere. In a scale of desirable qualities in those running a Home I would list character, personality and attitudes to people, problems, and life generally as more important than training. Wages and conditions need to be good, and work satisfaction is an important factor.

Originally the social worker took the patient to her new home, but at a later stage the procedure was changed and now the Matron comes to the hospital 'to take her home'. This arrangement has the added advantages of providing a basis for establishing a good relationship between the patient and the Matron, and it has strengthened very considerably the links between the hospital and the Home. The discussions which take place with the nursing staff on these visits is of course very helpful, and supplements the information given by the social worker.

The Matrons in private Homes have an advantage in that they can work as many hours as they choose and be fully flexible about staff, increasing at short notice the number on duty at any time or the number of hours worked.

Also important is the fact that the Matron contributes to the decision to receive the new resident. The involvement at this stage ensures a strong sense of responsibility and a real desire to succeed in the care of the new resident.

Matrons need to demonstrate and to set an example to their staff in the act of "caring" in the fullest sense. It is not a guarantee that nothing will go wrong but it does help to develop a strong sense of personal responsibility and a willingness to examine a situation when something has not worked out as had been hoped. A Home which has insufficient staff cannot provide the kind of care we have a right to expect. Meals and cups of tea seem nicer when they are served by someone who has time to be pleasant and knows individual likes and dislikes. The Matron and staff need to have time to do their work in such a way that they are able to give personal attention to the small but important things.

Once a relationship of mutual respect and trust has been established between the hospital and the Homes the departure of the patient from the hospital and the settling in period will take place with the minimum of stress. There is never any question of a Home reluctantly taking a patient. I am convinced that even fairly demented patients sense any feeling of rejection, whether it is by the family or by a Home. When removed from a rejecting environment the behaviour pattern of the patient often improves.

The Matron and her family running the Home, apart from assuming full responsibility, need to give of themselves and to be emotionally involved in their work. It is this which creates a home-like atmosphere and gives a feeling of continuity and security which is so desirable for the residents.

When the Matron has a family it adds an extra dimension for the residents and when there is a new baby it brings out a gentleness in the most unlikely residents which is quite remarkable. All ages in the family seem to make a contribution. A boy of 4 was often the only one who could get an 85-year old former Headmistress to go to the toilet; he took her. A girl of 9 plays chess and talks easily and happily with a former senior Civil Servant who presented many difficulties when he was in hospital and could silence most of us with a look.

When the Matron's family are older their styles of dress and way of life are a constant source of interest, it is the feeling of involvement which can be so valuable to the residents.

All the Matrons with young children or grandchildren say that they get spoilt by the reidents, they "gang up together". I am often surprised to find how very young children know the name of every resident.

When there is a family pet around, a cat or dog, it makes for a more homely atmosphere but as with the children the pets tend to get spoilt. Cats against all the rules quickly find which beds they are allowed on (or in), and instructions not to feed the dog are ignored.

Broadly speaking, in my view, younger long-stay patients leaving hospital who have no home of their own or relatives to go to need as a first priority a place not just to live in but one which will provide them with the kind of background which enables them to adjust to community life again. They need 'a mother figure' to encourage independence and initiative at the pace the patient can cope with. To try to find the right home and job for a patient straight from hospital generally brings too many pressures too quickly.

A considerable number of the patients I have been concerned with have gradually assumed responsibility for a domestic task in the Home for which they receive some payment. For those capable of some work but unable to work in a disciplined structure these arrangements work very well indeed. As you would expect however it creates some problems.

In one of the Homes visited regularly I quickly learnt not to put my cup down before I had finished the coffee, otherwise it was whipped away by as resident (a former long-stay patient) who was in charge of the cups. There was no question of changing the system. All visitors had to accept that they protected their own drinks.

Most people want to do things which they feel are useful and helpful and many remain caring towards others when they themselves are elderly and perhaps physically handicapped. Once the Matron and her staff recognise and appreciate the importance of these basic human needs their efforts are directed towards creating interest and opportunities for involvement by the residents in the day to day running of the Home. Striking the right balance between this and running the Home efficiently, is an art. It does not make for an easy way of life but when achieved it creates something of great value.

It is much easier and quicker to wash and dress a person who is very elderly and slow or handicapped than to enable her to wash and dress herself, or try to give thought to whether there is another acceptable resident who may welcome an opportunity to be helpful.

Quite recently a former younger patient who has been in the community for 16 years (she was previously in the hospital 12 years) had to go into a general hospital for surgery. She was visited regularly by the family running the home – she has no relatives – and on all their visits it came over clearly how much she was looking forward to getting home, the main reason being that she could take over again her self-selected task of "putting" an elderly resident to bed each evening.

It is so easy for all of us to fail to attach importance to simple every day matters which are in fact very important to the person concerned. I had many reminders that it was often very simple things which made all the difference.

Hospitals and other institutions need formal occupational therapy because they are such unnatural places to be in, but in the community, in my view, we should strive to involve former patients in normal living as far as possible and avoid an institutionalised approach. This calls for an imaginative approach by the Matrons.

During the last few years a number of Homes have had smoke detectors installed in each room. The general opinion is that apart from the occasions when they go off when the toast is burning, this addition to their home has brought great relief of mind, particularly during the night.

The work and responsibility of running a Registered Home appeals to many nurses and some of my nursing colleagues have gone into the possibilities of starting a Home. These enquiries have got no further than the Bank Manager. If it involves buying a property and a large mortgage it would be very difficult, particularly for the first year or more when income is not likely to cover outgoings. It takes time for a Home to become known and to build up a good reputation.

Many of the Homes under review started in a small way with an existing property and when they had gained confidence and knew that they liked the work they purchased a larger property, or in some instances bought the house next door.

For many reasons this gradual development is desirable. There is so much to learn and such a lot of demands are made on the person responsible. It takes time to get to know each new resident who may need considerable support for the first week or two; it is less easy to give this if several move in over a short period. By a policy of gradual Home improvement and extension acute financial worries can be avoided and inevitable delays in payments by the residents can be accepted without a fuss.

The need to introduce new residents into the Home gradually was demonstrated when a new ward was opened at the hospital and patients from many wards were transferred. The nursing staff were harrassed and unhappy; they found it difficult to get to know the patients as individuals, they were unable to give time to relatives, and in every way it was a disastrous start for a new ward. It took several months and a number of staff changes to get things running smoothly.

Registered Homes, like Psychiatric Hospitals, are very vulnerable. The people running the Homes need help in understanding the reasons for this, not only to enable them to cope with the situation themselves but so that they, in their turn, can help others to understand.

The Homes are open to a wide range of people – relatives and friends of the residents, G.Ps, Nurses, Local Authority Officers, Fire Officers, Social Workers, Ministers of Religion, DHSS Visiting Officers, representatives of Voluntary Organisations, Court of Protection visitors, traders and others, and the Matrons are aware of the desirability of establishing and maintaining good relationships with neighbours and the public at large. They are also very conscious of the need to respect the often conflicting rights and freedom between their residents and the public.

In one Home there are frequent skirmishes in the kitchen when a newcomer in all innocence takes on a job, i.e., putting the cups on the trolley, which is "work" that is done by another resident.

I mentioned dogs. One of these caused a punch up between three lady residents. Fortunately it took place in a country lane. The problem seemed to be that they each wanted to hold the lead. The Matron dealt with this by taking them around the lanes and marking the places where the change-over should be made, each having an equal share.

The Matron needs to accept that whilst being concerned with a group, the test of achievement or lack of it is judged and assessed by individual results. Every single resident may need care of some kind but they all need an environment in which they can feel as independent as possible and to create this it has to be thought about and planned.

Additionally she needs to recognize when a resident owing to the nature of her personality, her illness or the scars left by it is unable to adjust or change her ways in some particular circumstance.

Many Matrons make a point, where it seems indicated, of introducing a new resident to the local shop-keepers. The response shows that the effort is worth while and has been particularly helpful to former patients who may lack confidence or judgment when shopping. Publicans and "the man at the betting shop" have also been very kindly and helpful and many good relationships have been built up between residents of the Homes and local people.

It is unfortunate that the Homes which extend care to people who do not always conform are the very Homes which are likely to receive criticism. This in turn means that they are called upon in a very real way to help in changing public and sometimes official attitudes. All the Homes under review take in residents from other sources, e.g., through doctors, Health Visitors, Area Social Workers, relatives, etc. To say, as it has been said, that former psychiatric patients cannot share a home with others is nonsense. It depends entirely on the individual and the Home.

The D.H.S.S.

As 50% of the patients qualify for a supplementary pension or allowance there is a continuing contact with the DHSS, and in everybody's interest it is very desirable that there should be a good working relationships. There is a need for the local DHSS officers to understand the objectives of the scheme and its wide-reaching beneficial results, and there should be a willingness on both sides to examine and sort out problems as they arise.

When the Hospital and the DHSS have this positive approach, each accepting that they exist, within their own terms of reference, to help people, the financial aspects of the transfer of a patient from hospital to a new address in the community are made smoothly.

It is important that the DHSS is informed immediately of the change of address and circumstances. If it is a new application and not just a transfer, additional information at the time of the application will be helpful, e.g., next of kin, date of birth, previous address, etc., particularly when the patient may not have a good memory, or may not be able to answer a lot of questions. Some delay however is unavoidable, particularly with new applicants and this needs to be pointed out when using a Home for the first time as it can mean there is no payment until the first Giro or new book comes through. The established Homes accept the delays when they occur and it is helpful when they receive a 'phone' call from the visiting officer of the DHSS to pass on to the applicant the reason for an unusually long delay.

In one of the two DHSS Offices in the area covered by this survey one of the senior officers, was available to discuss any urgent or complicated problems. This was immensely helpful, especially the fact that after looking into the case he would 'phone back to give guidance or explain the situation. This enabled the social worker to pass on the information and often reassure an anxious applicant – an important point when concerned with someone who has just left hospital. This team-like approach kept problems and delays to a minimum and helped in the important work of developing good public relations.

The DHSS with its national structure, experience, expertise and machinery, all geared to dealing with payments to people, is ideally placed to handle the financial aspects of a scheme such as has been described. There is no red tape, no disclaiming responsibility because the applicant may have come from another area. The individual loses nothing of her identity and within the framework of financial restraints she has freedom of choice. Where there have been problems they have been due to human failures and not a weakness in the DHSS machinery. When a failure occurs (and this in my view is generally due to attitudes rather than mistakes) it can have very unfortunate results for the applicant – e.g. an elderly lady confined to a wheelchair and needing considerable care and attention was left penniless for over a year, despite the fact that all the circumstances were known to the DHSS. This former patient had no capital, property or income.

As indicated, the South Team covers two DHSS area offices. Both areas have very similar features e.g., they include seaside resorts, rural areas and high demand tourist centres but the level of supplementary allowance differs by £3 per week (at one time it was £5) for the same type of accommodation. It is not surprising that where the level of payments is higher there is a wider range of Homes and broadly speaking Homes of a higher standard. In this area there is an expressed recognition by the DHSS that enabling patients to leave hospital is socially desirable and economically sensible.

The Private Registered Homes fix their own charges and this needs to be understood by all concerned. The DHSS offices fix their level of allowances. In some areas in the country it has been so low that it has not allowed schemes of "finding homes" to get off the ground.

There is no hope of progress unless those prepared to make this service available feel that the return on investment and for their personal contribution is reasonably rewarded. This is compatible with the need to use public money in a responsible way. The cost of keeping patients in hospital is very much higher than care in a Registered Home. If we take the difference to be £40 per week – and this would be a modest estimate – the yearly average saving can be very considerable. It is wasteful of public money to keep people in hospital who do not need hospital care. The patient or relative or friend acting for her makes the decision about choice of Home. If the patient qualifies for a supplementary pension or allowance and chooses a Home where the charges are in excess of the total weekly income it needs to be explained before any pans are made that the differences will have to be made up in some way, e.g., by drawing on savings. Whilst some families have decided to make up the difference in order to enable a patient to go to a particular Home I would not feel it right to suggest this to them. In the same way, I would not try to persuade or press relations to have a patient to live with them if they showed no desire to do so. In the long term it would not be in the patient's interest.

The Role of the Social Worker

When an approach is made to a social worker about possible future plans for a patient it is getting down to details which is important, wherever the enquiry comes from and for whomsoever it is for. Handing out a list of Registered Homes is of little help; 90% of the Homes may be quite unsuitable for a particular person. Matching the individual to the Home is essential if we are to be concerned about happiness as well as care.

It has been suggested that finding homes in the community is a kind of welfare job, a sort of second grade social work. It is this kind of approach and misjudgment that can lead to very unsatisfactory results. It is better that the work is not attempted if the full implications are not appreciated or the right social worker is not available. The prime motive of the social worker must be to find the best available Home for the patient. Releasing a hospital bed is the bonus.

In my experience Matrons like most of us, respond well to the need and expectation of high standards of caring. It implies a feeling of sharing a responsibility and is an important factor in the development of the high regard which the Homes have for the work of the hospital.

The social worker's role is to be available for guidance and support. The major responsibility for the care and happiness of the patient rests with those who are running the Home, and it is most important that nothing should be done to undermine this feeling of responsibility.

It does not follow that because a Home is registered it is suitable for patients. The attitude of the Matron and staff may be too rigid (it isn't numbers which create an institutional atmosphere!) or they may be incapable of coping with the kind of situation which can occur with the mentally frail, or there may be too much supervision when the need is an environment which fosters a spirit of independence.

Additionally, the social worker needs to be concerned to see that those providing "care" receive a fair and reasonable payment. A guide to what is reasonable can perhaps be based on what it would cost the Local Authority to provide a similar service. On this basis the low level of payments in some areas for fostering children is disgraceful.

In a B.B.C. interview a Senior Social Worker was appealing for foster parents and during the programme he implied that he was looking for people who were not interested in the money side. If this really is a sound policy perhaps we ought to try to recruit social workers and others on the same basis. A Senior DHSS Officer when discussing Private Registered Homes said "we must remember they are doing it for profit." I gathered he was helping the poor and the sick not for any monetary gain but just because he liked to be helpful.

Preparation for the patient leaving hospital is very important and particularly for those patients who have been in hospital a year or more. Things like spectacles, hearing aids, teeth or dentures etc. need checking in good time. New clothing and footwear are often needed, and the patient as far as possible should select this herself, or indicate the colour and kind of garments she likes. She will need a tooth-brush, comb, face cloth, cash, her pension book, etc., and a hair-do will need to be arranged.

These things are obviously very important to the patient and additionally they set an example of "caring". It demonstrates that when a large Institution is divided into smaller units where there is a unified policy it can be caring in a very personal way. It needs good team work between the social worker and nursing staff.

Many of the Matrons have commented on how nice patients have looked when they come to pick them up from hospital. In the early days of the scheme (1962) patients were always turned out clean but so often in ill-fitting and unbecoming clothes. A senior nurse told me that it was "a waste of money for some of the patients to have new clothing".

The Social Worker in my view needs to set an example to the Homes of "caring" in the widest sense. Finding a home for someone is not just a case of a bed and food, important as these things are. It is finding somewhere where that person can be helped to live as full and happy a life as possible whatever the level might be.

As the role of the social worker is to *help a patient find a suitable home,* the approach needs to be dynamic and positive. If approached with a view to releasing a hospital bed the scheme would break down. It is the thought which goes into *helping each patient as an individual* and preparing the home to receive her which makes it work. There can be no justification for the medical and nursing staff of a psychiatric hospital devoting all their skills to helping a patient if she is to be discharged to an environment which is unsuitable. If the home were not selected carefully to meet the patient's emotional and material needs, it would simply mean unhappiness for the patient and a high rate of re-admissions.

We have a right to expect a high level of "caring" if we as social workers demonstrate what we mean by this – it is a powerful guide line. It leads to the maximum time being available to the actual work of helping people and to the minimum of time compatible with efficient administration being given to form filling. It is a guarantee to a clash with bureaucracy.

There are many patients' files containing lengthy social worker notes and involving correspondence and visits, and at the end of it all the patient remains in exactly the same position. The kind of help needed has not been given.

In my view, social workers should be more willing to ask themselves at the end of the day "how have I been helpful to the patient or client?" and to accept that we will be judged to a large extent by results. To show evidence of effort and time spent on a problem is not enough, impressive as this may be.

In those cases when it applies, the social worker in order to protect and help the patient, the hospital, the person acting for the patient and the home which is going to be involved needs to have a thorough grasp of the implications of Power of Attorney and Receivership Orders under the Court of Protection.

In discussing the question of priorities in loyalty at a meeting it was expressed as "loyalty to immediate colleagues, Area Office and County Hall in that order". I believe as hospital social workers our first priority should be for the patient and that we should also feel a strong sense of concern for the functioning of the hospital. If these priorities lead to conflict perhaps we ought to be willing to examine the situation more fully.

The Relatives

The image of an institution dies hard and the hospital still admits patients who express fears that they will never be allowed to leave – they need and receive reassurance. Occasionally relatives seek reassurance on this point but sometimes it is the other way about; they had assumed when the patient was admitted that she would be staying in hospital for life, and when the position is explained to them their reaction is one of disappointment and sometimes anger. They may have had a difficult and worrying time prior to the patient's admission and feel unable to take on the same responsibilities again. In these circumstances the heat and stress can be taken out of the situation by explaining that full help will be extended by the hospital with regard to discharge arrangements. Relatives can be made aware that they will not be pressurised into taking on more than they feel able to cope with. What seems particularly reassuring to relatives is to be told that the social worker will be maintaining contact with the patient for as long as seems necessary after she has left the hospital. It avoids the fear that they may have of being 'landed again'.

There is another kind of relative – the one who wants the patient to stay in hospital because there is no charge. In these cases the social worker can expect problems and is not exactly popular, but this should not be allowed to result in the patient staying in hospital longer than is necessary.

This kind of case tends to stick in one's mind but they are in the minority. Most relatives who we see are nearly at breaking point themselves as a result of caring, night and day, over a long period for a loved one. My experience is that the great majority of immediate relatives extend help to the best of their ability but I accept that ability levels vary a good deal.

The approach by the social worker in these circumstances needs to be helpful and firm, and the Team policy needs to be explained. Putting the patient's name on a waiting list for a Home where the waiting period might be many months or even years is no way of dealing with the situation. What is essential is that the social worker has specific suggestions to put forward for the patient's care.

Many relatives find it difficult to understand or accept the effect of senile dementia on a patient. They say "but she was so clever" or "she was always such a good person". They always hope for a cure. This inability by a relative to accept the situation (and it applies particularly at the onset of the patient's illness) can create a difficult situation when the patient returns home. Her memory loss may lead to many problems and cause considerable stress to the relative who may feel in turn both angry and guilty.

Looking to the Future

For the forseeable future there will be a continuing and increasing need for private Homes which provide a caring service, good standards at a reasonable charge and have the ability to cope.

On a number of occasions the Registered Homes have been used for holiday periods to give a relative the opportunity of a break, and also as day places to enable a patient to return home to a working relative. There is scope for considerable development in these areas of social need.

A number of hospitals in other areas have sought our help in enabling one of their patients to come into this area to be near to a relative.

In my view there is a need for a wide range of Registered Homes which are not categorised, i.e., by age or disability. Experience has shown that Homes with a mixed age group and people with varying degrees of disability – mental and physical – can function very well indeed and in this kind of environment those needing help themselves can often find an opportunity of helping others.

We have a right to expect far more from our Registered Homes than the mere compliance with Regulations, and Officers can play a part in encouraging constantly rising standards.

Local Authorities through their Part 111 accommodation need to develop and demonstrate to a greater extent that they can care for a wider range of elderly people. I am referring to the considerable number who do not need hospital care but by the nature of their problems are difficult to look after in an ordinary family home, e.g., those who:—

1. need help with washing, dressing, toileting, etc.

2. are confused and perhaps tend to wander

3. refuse to conform

4. suffer from delusions, hallucinations or depression but on medical opinion do not need hospitalization

5. have a drink problem

6. are incontinent. It is often on this problem alone that relatives feel they cannot cope.

These are the people who call for an imaginative approach, considerable skills and individual attention.

A considerable number of residents from Part III accommodation have been admitted to hospital as the Matrons felt unable to provide the kind of care required. Many of these have been discharged to private Registered Homes and have settled without too many problems.

Perhaps Local Authorities should recruit more staff with psychiatric nursing experience for work in their Homes. There is a need to accept the challenge of caring for the non-conformers and all that it implies. The emphasis needs to be on meeting a social need in a very individual way and the administrative side should be geared to this. It should lead to less form filling and a more imaginative and bold approach.

In the development of their work Local Authorities are limited by financial restrictions. One of the important factors in the development of a scheme of finding Homes in the private sector is that no capital investment is required from either the State or the Local Authority.

In many areas there are demands for more beds in hospitals for geriatric patients, yet in some of these same areas there are patients in hospitals who do not need hospital care. They need help in finding a suitable place in the community. Hospitals need to press for a service which meets the needs of patients who cannot return to their admission address. The challenge to the social worker concerned with the elderly, the mentally frail or handicapped, or children, is to find these people, to recognise their qualities, and to help them to use and develop them in the interests of the community.

In addition to the need for hospitals to develop this kind of service for their patients there is an equally important need for community-based schemes where those concerned with the elderly, the handicapped, etc., can seek help and advice on care and accommodation problems. Councils of Social Service or similar organisations, given adequate financial support and with their wide experience and absence of bureaucracy, are well placed to take on this kind of service.

APPENDIX 1

Survey (July 1969) of Patients Discharged to Five Homes

Patient's Age	No. of Previous Admissions	Over No. of Years	Total Period in Hospital (years)	Date of Discharge	No. of Adms. since New Accom.	Medical
70	1	$\frac{1}{4}$	1/6	1964	—	Chronic schizophrenic paranoid type.
68	—	36	33	1962	2	Chronic schizophrenia – arterio sclerotic brain damage now.
86	—	—	21	1964	—	Paranoid Psychosis – schizophrenia.
68	1	13	6	1964	—	Organic syndrome – G.P.I.
67	2	3	$1\frac{1}{2}$	1967	1	Depression/Borderline sub-normal Paranoid features/ Epilepsy.
52	7	8	4	1966	—	Epileptic psychosis/sub-normality.
72	2	4	$1\frac{1}{2}$	1966	—	Said to have dementia, Epilepsy and congestive heart failure.
76	—	—	16	1966	—	Medical assessment appears to have been wrong in early stages of illness, could well have been a neurotic of some severity, but was said to suffer from "Senile dementia" when only 56.
79	—	—	$\frac{1}{2}$	1967	—	Arteriosclerotic dementia.
74	6	12	2	1966	—	Manic depressive syndrome.
60	—	—	24	1968	—	Organic syndrome; aetiology.
64	—	—	9	1968	—	Diagnosis never really established, neurosis, Myxoedemia, Dementia.
69	2	5	1/6	1968	—	Recurrent depression.
66	—	—	15	1968	—	Probable excited paranoid schizophrenia.
83	—	—	$\frac{1}{4}$	1969	—	Senile dementia.
45	—	—	9	1962	—	Chronic schizophrenia.
67	—	—	$24\frac{1}{2}$	1963	3	Paranoid psychosis. Re-admitted due to extra-pyramidal effects of treatment.
82	—	—	1/12	1967	—	Dementia; aetiology.
66	2	3	7/12	1968	—	Paraphrenia.
83	1	25	24	1969	—	Probable schizophrenic relapse.
59	—	—	5/12	1968	—	Alcoholism, some brain damage.
54	3	28	$24\frac{1}{2}$	1966	—	Probably subnormal, depressive.

173

Patient's Age	No. of Previous Admissions	Over No. of Years	Total Period in Hospital (years)	Date of Discharge	No. of Adms. since New Accmd.	Medical
82	1	4	1	1967	—	A.S. Dementia.
68	—	—	31	1966	—	G.P.I.
68	—	—	42	1969	—	Chronic schizophrenic.
79	2	13	8½	1969	—	Recurrent depression.
65	—	—	30	1966	—	Chronic schizophrenic.
66	2	13	9½	1966	—	Chronic schizophrenic.
67	1	38	14½	1966	—	Chronic schizophrenic.
69	—	—	18	1966	—	Schizophrenia. Mania.
80	1	1½	1½	1965	—	Chlorodyne addict, chronic schizo, Leucotomy.
54	5	15	12	1967	—	Subnormal. Depressive syndrome. Paranoid state-Hypotensive (severe) E.C.T.
76	1	22	22	1967	—	Congestive heart failure, deafness symptomatic psychosis.
70	—	—	3/12	1968	—	Alcoholism/Mild dementia.
52	—	—	15	1963	—	Subnormal.
66	—	—	33	1963	—	Chronic schizophrenic.
73	—	—	2	1966	—	Chronic paranoid psychosis.
83	—	—	8/12	1967	—	Depressive syndrome.
66	—	—	4/12	1969	—	Agitated depression.
65	—	—	39	1963	—	Chronic schizophrenic.
71	—	—	1/2	1969	—	Chronic schizophrenic.
78	—	—	34	1969	—	Chronic schizophrenic.
61	—	—	29	1969	—	Chronic schizophrenic.
66	—	—	31	1969	—	Probable schizophrenia now dementing.
83	1	19	2½	1966	—	Endogenous depression.
89	2	16	7	1966	—	Depressive syndrome/Senile dementia.
88	—	—	29½	1969	—	Chronic schizophrenic.
68	1	8/12	3/12	1968	—	Endogenous depressive.
65	1	3	2½	1969	—	Endogenous depressive.
84	—	—	1/12	1969	—	Endogenous depressive.

PART SEVEN

THE ROLE
OF THE LOCAL
AUTHORITY

10: Services for the Mentally Ill —
A Local Authority Perspective
Tom White and Alan Holden

Summary

The modern approach to mental illness relies heavily on care in the community. The major responsibility for providing community care rests on local authority social services departments. Local authorities have been the subject of much criticism for their "failure" to meet adequately the demand for community care. In this paper we examine the extent to which local health authorities were able to develop community services between 1960 and 1971, and the progress made by social services departments since that date. In spite of the major re-organisations which have affected the personal social services – in 1971 and again in 1974 – and the very difficult economic circumstances of the last few years, the achievements of local authorities are considerable. Local authority expenditure on personal social services for the mentally ill more than doubled in real terms from 1972 to 1977, and there was a 50% increase in residential provision in the same period.

The factor determining the rate of progress is not the commitment of local authorities, but the constraints on capital development imposed by Central Government. Even with these constraints progress is being made more quickly than was foreseen by the 1975 White Paper "Better Services for the Mentally Ill". Given the necessary resources social services departments would be able to accelerate the improvement of these services.

Introduction

The Mental Health Act 1959 gave statutory recognition to the fundamental changes in attitude and approach to the treatment of mental illness which had been taking place in the preceding decade. At the same time as the Act was implemented, directions under the National Health Service Act placed new duties on local authorities to provide for the care and after-care outside hospitals of people who suffered from mental illness. The profound change in philosophy which had given rise to the 1959 Act was in the direction of treatment and care in the local community and it was to be the services provided by local authorities which would be the foundation of "community care" as an alternative to isolation in hospitals.

The duties of local authorities with social services responsibilities towards people who are suffering, or who have suffered, from mental illness are wide ranging, but contain a large element of discretion. Local authorities may provide residential care, day care and such ancillary services as they think are needed in their areas.[1] The Secretary of State for Social Services has given general approval for the provision of services of this kind for the mentally ill[2], but the power of the Secretary of State to give directions, and make the provision of services mandatory, has never been exercised.

Nearly twenty years have passed since the watershed of the 1959 Act, long enough away for attention to focus on its deficiencies; its advantages are now taken for granted. It is a fact that the intervening years have not seen the blossoming of community care to nothing like the extent which is needed to provide a viable alternative to hospital based treatment. It has been said elsewhere[3] that "the failure, for which central government as much as local government is responsible, to develop anything approaching adequate social services is perhaps the greatest disappointment" of the period since the Act. The frustration of the medical professions, who see the lack of community care as preventing them from offering effective treatment to their patients, with this situation is understandable and shared by social workers and senior staff of local authorities.

The questions which must now be addressed concern the commitment of local authorities to the community care, and the future prospects for the provision the community services which should have come into existence fifteen or more years ago.

Local Authority Provision

There was virtually no community care provision by local authorities when the Mental Health Act was implemented in 1960. For the first ten years or so responsibility for making appropriate services available to the mentally ill rested on the Health Departments of County and County Borough Councils. In 1971 responsibility was transferred on their establishment to the Social Services Departments of local authorities, as part of the amalgamation of the personal social services.

Although one might have expected local health departments to have been in sympathy with and committed to the concept of community care, the establishment of the necessary community services for the mentally ill was undertaken very slowly. In more recent years, since the services became the concern of social services departments, provision has been undertaken more enthusiastically, in spite of the economic crises which have beset the country and the restraint on local authority spending which has been imposed as a result.

The table below illustrates the development of residential and day care services from zero provision in 1960, and the national targets which have been suggested by the Secretary of State for the level of service required.

Table 1

Residential and Day Care for the Mentally Ill —
Provision by Local Authorities:

	March 1972	March 1977	Targets
Residential Care:			
Total places provided	2,016	3,092	12,100
Proportion of authorities with provision	50%	85%	100%
Day Care:			
Total places provided	2,832	3,679*	29,600
Proportion of authorities with provision	33%	51%	100%

	1972/73	*1977/78*	*1981/82*
Expenditure on services:	*Actual*	*Estimate*	*Projection*
Price Base	Out-turn	Nov. '76	Nov. '76
Total expenditure	£2.4m	£10.8m	£17m
Proportion of LA spending on social services	0.74%	1.05%	1.7%
Expenditure/1,000 population aged 18-64 on:			
Residential Care	£54	£246	£270
Day Care	£29	£128	£300

* March 1976 figure.

Note:
Data on the provision of places relates to England only: financial data relates to expenditure in England and Wales. The figures have been drawn from a number of sources: existing provision from DHSS Feedback Tables; targets from DHSS Circular 35/72; expenditure levels from CIPFA (IMTA) Social Services Statistics; expenditure projection from DHSS Planning Guidelines 1978/79.

It has been suggested by some parts of the medical profession that the continued shortage of community care facilities is somehow a consequence of the creation of social services departments, and that the mentally ill would have fared rather better if responsibility for their particular services had not been included among those given to the new departments. On the contrary the evidence in Table 1 clearly illustrates that services for the mentally ill have benefited substantially from inclusion in the responsibilities of local social services authorities.

The provision of alternative residential accommodation is one of the key elements necessary to reduce the demand for in-patient treatment. In the 12 years up to March 1972 only 2,000 of the 12,000 places needed had been provided by local health authorities. In the next 5 years to March 1977 more than a thousand additional places were added to the total available in England. By 1977 only 15% of all authorities did not have any kind of residential provision, whereas residential care had been available in only half of all local authority areas in 1972.

Comparison of the amounts of money spent on day and residential care services for the mentally ill shows even more clearly the investment in such services undertaken by social services departments. There was a four-fold increase in expenditure on these services between 1972/73 and 1977/78. Some of this was due to the effects of inflation. To allow for this we can calculate the equivalent of £2.4m on the price base of the 1977/78 figures, which turns out to be £5.1m. Thus in five years spending on day and residential care for the mentally ill more than doubled *in real terms.* The share of the total local authority social services budget which this represents rose from 0.74% to 1.05%. These are both very small percentages, but they illustrate the efforts which social services departments are making to improve on the very inadequate service which they inherited.

It has apparently not proved possible for social services departments to improve on the rate of development of day care which was achieved by local health authorities. In any case it is our view that statistics on day care should be treated with caution as they do not convey a complete picture of the service available. It is not clear in published statistics how many places are available full-time (i.e. all day, five days a week) and which only part-time. Nor do they completely take account of the modern trend to increasingly provide day care in multi-purpose centres catering for more than one client group. In March 1976 there were in England 179 of these centres, offering over 11 thousand places. It is known that at least 300 of these places are set aside for the mentally ill (which have been included in the figure for day care provision at March 1976 in the table), but it is possible that considerably more places may be utilised for the benefit of the mentally ill without being explicitly reserved for them.

180

Social work services within many departments are now provided on a generic basis, so it is no longer possible to identify specific social workers as being exclusively concerned with the mentally ill, as was formerly the case. In general there has been a substantial growth in the availability of social work help. For example in 1972 there were 12,700 staff employed in fieldwork within social services departments; by 1977 it is estimated that this number had grown to 23,000.[4] This is a very substantial increase in the provision of social workers and other social work staff, which will have benefited all client groups, including the mentally ill.

Progress in spite of constraints

Most local authorities, through their social services departments, are fully committed to the adequate provision of community care for the mentally ill. As we have shown, considerable progress has already been made to expand the services which we inherited in 1971. Clearly there is still a considerable way to go until a really satisfactory service is attained. Before looking at the prospects of doing so, it is as well to remind ourselves of the two major upheavals to which local authority social services have been subjected in recent years.

Firstly there was the actual formation of local authority social services departments in 1971, which arose directly from the acceptance by Parliament of the major recommendations of the Seebohm Committee. This Committee had been established in 1965 with terms of reference ". . . to review the organisation and responsibilities of the local authority personal social services . . . and to consider what changes are desirable to secure an effective family service."[5] The Committee found that the existing system of fragmented responsibility for different aspects of the personal social services unsatisfactory for six basic reasons:—

1. Inadequacies in the amount of provision, with long waiting lists for most services;
2. Inadequacies in the range of services, whose fragmented nature tended to produce separate spheres of responsibility with neglected areas in between;
3. Inadequacies in the quality of provision – old buildings and a lack of properly trained staff;
4. Poor co-ordination;
5. Difficult access;
6. Insufficient flexibility and adaptability.

The Committee recommended that a new, family orientated, community based service, sensitive to local needs, should be established in each local authority area. The Committee saw that one of the principal causes of the deficiencies, in the services it studied, was the inability of the fragmented services to attract sufficient resources to themselves. In consequence the greater ability to attract resources which would be possessed by a large, integrated, department was one of the major arguments in favour of fundamental change[6]. As has already been seen, resources in terms of manpower have increased markedly. The proportion of local authority spending devoted to the personal social services has also risen significantly. In 1972/73, 5.8% of local authority expenditure in Great Britain was devoted to the personal social services. In 1977/78 the proportion was 7.4%, and by 1981/82 it is expected to have risen to 7.7%.[7] The only other areas of expenditure where the share of total spending has risen are education (45.0% in 72/73, 45.6% in 77/78, but expected to be only 44.2% in 81/82) and law enforcement (8.5%, 9.8% and 9.6% respectively). In our view the increased consciousness of social problems which social services departments have been able to generate within local authorities has played a major role in securing this increased share of resources.

More adequate resources and a greater availability of staff are not the only benefits of the Seebohm re-organisation which the mentally ill, along with other client groups, have enjoyed. The integration of the various aspects of the personal social services has made possible a holistic approach to the problems of mental illness, an end to the serious problems which stemmed from ignoring the wider aspects of the client's situation, and from them not knowing where to turn for help outside the limited purview of the mental welfare officer. An integrated service opens up to the mentally ill person the possibility of access to the whole range of resources which the local authority can offer such help can take account of every aspect of the ill person's social needs and those of his family, and there is much less risk that stigma will arise from receiving help from a 'generic' social services department. Many of the social needs of the mentally ill are of a general kind, and an individual's social problem may be the route by which an associated mental illness, not previously identified by the medical services, may come to light.

Co-operation between local authority services and the National Health Service is a further area in which re-organisation has benefited the mentally ill. Joint financing, which will undoubtedly accelerate the provision of facilities for those affected by mental illness, is the most obvious facet of the relationship which has been fostered between social services departments and Area and District Health Authorities. The joint provision of services, consultation and joint planning which is now taking place is much greater than would have been the case between local health authorities and hospital management committees prior to re-organisation.

Co-operation has also been enhanced by another consequence of integration. The social services departments have been able to provide the necessary framework for social workers to develop greater independence of judgement. The concept of a multi-disciplinary team assumes a more significant meaning and the contribution of the professional social worker to the team is enhanced.

The accessability of services to potential clients was a particular concern of the Seebohm Committee, who recommended "one door" through which potential clients could gain access to the whole range of services.[8] The pattern of organisation which has been adopted almost universally by social services departments is to have local district or area offices, which act as the bases for local social work teams. In this way the social work services can be known in their local area, people have less problem in knowing where to go to seek help, and there is now no question of potential clients having to guess in advance the right place to go with their particular kind of need. Nor are potential clients deterred by the practical problems of travelling to a distant, city centre office lost in the midst of Town or County Hall.

For example in Coventry, where there was once one mental health department office in a large city centre council office building containing many other City Council departments, we plan a network of local social services centres, each serving a population of around 20,000 people. These centres will be in local shopping centres and other focal points in the neighbourhood. This network is already two thirds complete and we have found there is a dramatic increase in the readiness of people to seek help when there is a clear, unambiguous source of advice which is local. This experience is by no means unique, but has been repeated in many different areas.

There were of course some disadvantages in the re-organisation of the personal social services, which were essentially short term in nature. Many individual relationships which had grown up between medical and social work staff were ruptured as a consequence of the changes in responsibility experienced by individual social workers. There was inevitably a dilution for a time of the specialised skills which had been built up over a number of years. The problems this created were real, but temporary. It also seems to us that much of the anxiety about the loss of the mental welfare officer as a separate entity was over concern with his role in compulsory admission procedures to hospital, and did not give adequate recognition of his role in treatment and rehabilitation.

The second major upheaval of the personal social services arose out of the re-organisation of local government itself (outside London) in 1974. This resulted in fundamental changes for the majority of authorities with social services responsibilities, and imposed a further period of disruption, with consequent temporary deterioration in the standards of service available, on a service which was just recovering from the dislocation caused by the earlier re-organisation. In the long run this second re-organisation will also bring benefits to social services users, including the mentally ill, by providing a really comprehensive range of services.

The period through which social services departments have expanded provision for the mentally ill has not been an easy one for local government. The economic climate within which services have been operating could hardly have been more bleak. Because of the crisis triggered off by the rise in the price of oil, balance of payments deficits and very high rates of inflation, stringent economies in public spending were announced in 1975. These economies resulted in a £3 billion reduction in the public expenditure plans for the years to 1978/79: health and personal social services contributing £150 million to this sum. That services have continued to grow throughout this period must be to the credit of local authorities, and demonstrates their commitment to improving facilities for the mentally ill.

A Review of Progress

The Government reviewed progress in the development of services for the mentally ill in a White Paper published in 1975.[9] The White Paper re-affirmed the view that community care is the right philosophical approach, and discussed how it could become more of a reality. The Government embodied in the White Paper its commitment to a strategy designed to make community care the principal method of responding to psychiatric illness.[10] The strategy outlined has four main elements.

The first element, and perhaps the most important, is an expansion of local authority personal social services to provide greater residential, domiciliary, day care and social work support for the mentally ill. The Government is now committed to a substantial expansion of these services "as soon as economic circumstances permit."[11] The second element is the relocation to local settings

184

of the specialist services within the N.H.S. more usually found in remote psychiatric hospitals. Thirdly there is the establishment of better co-ordination between the various services for the mentally ill; and lastly the final element of the Government's strategy is a significant improvement in staffing to provide for multi-disciplinary assessment of patients' individual needs and for greater emphasis on early intervention and prevention.

The first of these elements is, as we have shown, being undertaken vigorously by local authorities to the limits of the constraints placed upon them. Spending in real terms on day and residential care has doubled in the last five years – representing an annual rate of growth of 15%. If the momentum of recent years can be sustained – very largely a political decision by central government – the targets for the provision of residential care will be achieved in a further 16 years. If economic circumstances improve and central government can allocate more resources to social services departments progress could be made more quickly still. While this is not in the immediate future, 16 years is considerably quicker than was envisaged in the 1975 White Paper, which saw 20 to 30 years as an acceptable time scale for the establishment of the new pattern of services.[12] At present rates of progress the achievement of the day care target will take rather longer, but again would be significantly faster if there were improved financial support by central Government.

It is understandable that both patients, their families and staff, including social workers, should experience feelings of frustration when contemplating the length of time which must elapse before a fully comprehensive community care service can become a reality. If existing services were run down before a viable alternative is available chaos and hardship for patients would ensue. The Government has made it plain that this will not happen. An existing mental hospital will not be closed until a range of alternative facilities is available throughout its catchment area, and it is no longer needed for long-stay patients admitted to its care before local services came into operation.[13]

Accelerated Provision

Would it be possible to speed up the provision of the local authority services required to implement the philosophy of community care? If we are to find a way of doing so two crucial issues must be faced; finding the necessary resources, and the willingness of the community to accept rapid change in methods of dealing with psychiatric illness. Let us look at the question of resources first.

Local authorities do not have a free hand in determining how much they should spend. The Government, through the rate support grant, exercises considerable influence over the total amount spent each year by local authorities. It has been suggested[14] that the overall running costs of the new pattern of services, taking local authority and health services together, will be no greater than the running costs of the existing services, although clearly there will in the long run be a substantial transfer of responsibility for financing services from the health service to local authorities. The conclusion that overall running costs will not rise is open to considerable doubt. It appears to make no allowance for improvements in the standard of care, which will inevitably increase unit costs, and offset the effect in the hospital service of falling numbers. The conclusion also appears to overlook the fourth element of the Government's declared strategy – the increases of skilled staff needed by diagnostic and preventive services. However, if we accept for the moment that overall running costs will not change, and the necessary mechanisms can be set up to effect the required transfer of resources from the health service to local authorities, there is still the problem of the substantial capital investment needed in new buildings.

In the personal social services the central Government exercises fairly direct control over the amount of capital development undertaken for each client group, through the use of key sector loan sections. The Government determines both the overall total of capital expenditure it will permit in each year, and the balance of projects between the various client groups, although the final package of projects across the nation as a whole will be influenced by the requests submitted by local authorities. The White Paper acknowledged that many local authorities could point to capital schemes which would have benefited the mentally ill for which loan sanction had been refused.[15]

The limits on capital spending at the moment are very stringent. In the current year (1978/79) authorities may spend in general no more than 80p per head of population on capital spending for the social services of all kinds.[16] In recent years this limit has been as low as 60p. The indications are that the current limit will apply for at least one further year. There is as yet no clear indication that the limit will be raised substantially, although it must be if local authorities are to be free to provide the facilities they know are urgently needed in their areas.

There are some tentative indications that the need to relax this aspect of central Government control over local authority action. The latest planning guidelines for local authority social services spending[17] include an "illustrative projection" for total social services capital spending in 1981/82 of £68 million (in England and Wales). The existing limit is around £40 million, and the capital part of the joint financing programme cannot account for all the difference.

The White Paper of 1975 recognised that considerable capital development would be needed. The amount required was estimated at £8 million annually for a minimum of 20 years.[18] Planning guidelines for the health and personal social services published shortly afterwards[19] indicated that local authorities should plan to increase their capital spending on facilities for the mentally ill from £2 million in 75/76 to £7 million in 79/80 (all at 1974 prices). The most recent planning guidelines have suggested that capital spending on mental illness facilities should now reach £11 million by 1981/82, and that there should be 10% growth on current spending on residential care and 19% growth in current spending on day care for the mentally ill. It remains to be seen whether authorities will be given the resources to achieve these targets. It should also be noted that 10% growth in current spending on residential care is less than has been achieved in the last five years. This would seem to suggest that improved day care should be pursued at the expense of residential care for the mentally ill, a totally unacceptable proposition.

But if greater resources are not found for the personal social services, improvements in one aspect of provision can by and large only be achieved by taking money and manpower away from another aspect. We must rob Peter to pay Paul! One of the most difficult tasks facing local authorities is that of choosing between conflicting priorities. We are advised to concentrate our efforts only on those parts of our services which should be accorded priority. But every single facet of local authority personal social services has been identified as deserving high priority for development. How does a local authority make meaningful choices between, for example promoting services for the elderly, providing for children in need, or supporting the mentally ill?

One way out of the dilemma would be for the massive transfer of resources from the health service to local authority personal social services promised in the White Paper to become a reality. Local authorities are most anxious to see some commitment being given by the Government that such a transfer will take place. There is a genuine fear that savings arising from falling numbers of patients in psychiatric hospitals will be retained in the NHS to pay for improved care for the remaining patients. This is already official policy in relation to the mentally handicapped[20], and could easily become so for the mentally ill.

The existing arrangements for joint financing between health and local authorities is a step in the right direction and a welcome injection of funds. It is however a relatively modest scheme which, in its present form, can only make marginal improvements to local authority services. The scheme as it is at present structured has two major limitations. An allocation of funds has only been announced for three years ahead – a relatively short time in the context of the time scale needed for the overall development of services. Secondly the scheme involves local authorities in accepting long term responsibility for the running costs of each project started under joint financing, at the end of a five or seven year period during which responsibility is shared. Some local authorities have been reluctant to take up their full allocation of joint financing, as they could not guarantee they would have adequate resources available at the right time to fulfil these commitments.

It is sometimes suggested that provision could easily be accelerated by adopting "low-cost" solutions, such as meeting accommodation needs in supervised lodgings. While such schemes should be, and are being, investigated and implemented, we do not think that low cost schemes can be other than a minor contribution to meeting overall need. To follow up the example of supervised lodgings; in many areas of the country, particularly in urban areas where there is already an acute shortage of accommodation for single people, it would not be possible to find sufficient placements to make an appreciable impact on the needs of the mentally ill for special accommodation. We would also suggest that, given the market cost of lodgings, enhanced payments to landladies to recognise the responsibility they would be accepting, and the degree of social work support which would be needed in a properly established scheme of supervised lodgings, the financial savings which would result, compared with needs, e.g. hostels or group homes, would be much less than is sometimes envisaged.

We must also recognise that any expansion of community care is dependent on the availability of suitable social work staff, both field and residential, with appropriate training. That too ultimately depends on money, and any consideration of financial issues must include the question of staff and training, the mere provision of buildings is not enough. The scheme of special government aid to services for the mentally ill which we advocate below would have to include adequate finance to train staff for the new services, and to provide the field social work and other domiciliary services which would form an integral part of the new pattern of services.

Local authorities who wish to see a rapid improvement in services for the mentally ill find themselves in a "Catch 22" situation if they do not wish to impoverish all their other services. It is clearly right that existing health services should not be run down until alternatives in the ommunity are

188

available. Assuming that resources are eventually to be switched to local authorities, they can only be taken away from the health service after there has been a fall in the number of psychiatric patients in hospitals. That fall in numbers can only occur when local authorities provide much more day and residential care for the mentally ill. This can only be accomplished rapidly if additional resources are given to local authorities; and Government policy is that these resources must come from the health service. There is only one way to break into the circle, and that is for the Government to give sufficient additional funds to local authorities now, specifically for services for the mentally ill, in the expectation that they will in due course be offset by savings in the health services. Precedents are available allowing the Government to allocate money for specific uses without threatening the autonomy of local authorities – for example in housing and education, and within the social services field grants for secure accommodation and joint financing itself.

However, even if the financial problems can be solved there would be other difficulties in the way of a rapid expansion of community care, focussed on the willingness or otherwise of the community to accept the mentally ill in their midst. The policies of segregation practised over the last hundred years have left a legacy of ignorance and fear surrounding mental illness in the minds of the general public which is not easily overcome. Our experience in Coventry, which we do not think is different from that of other authorities, has been that without exception every proposal for the provision of some facility for the mentally ill has been met by strong opposition from residents of the neighbourhood where the facility is to be sited. It is not unknown for the opposition in some regrettable cases to be led by local elected members of the same authority which was trying to fulfil its duty to meet the needs of the mentally ill in its area by providing the facility. So often the arguments in which the opposition is couched show, by emphasising the "risks" to which the children of the neighbourhood might be "exposed", the profound lack of understanding about mental illness which is commonly found among the lay public.

We have found that the fears and anxieties of local people can be allayed by careful preparation and much patient explanation of the true nature of psychiatric illness and its effects. The necessity to undertake this preparation would limit the rapidity with which an expansion of community care could take place, even if money were available in unlimited quantities. We would suggest that the Government should consider the advisability mounting a central campaign to educate the public about the needs of the mentally ill and the contribution which the community can make to their treatment and rehabilitation.

Conclusion

It is difficult to generalise about local authorities, and we would readily accept that isolated authorities have not done all they could to provide community services for the mentally ill. The great majority of local authorities are firmly committed to the principles of community care and are promoting the development of services as rapidly as circumstances permit. Only action by Central Government can accelerate the provision of community resources and bring about the pattern of services envisaged in the 1975 White Paper in less than the 15-20 years which current trends suggest is the minimum period before such an end can be achieved.

References

1. Schedule 8 to the *National Health Service Act 1977.*
2. D.H.S.S. Local Authority Circular 19/74.
3. *Better Services for the Mentally Ill,* Cmnd 6233, HMSO 1975; paragraph 2.8.
4. *CIPFA Social Services Statistics;* Actuals 1972/3 and Estimates 1977/78.
5. *Report of the Committee on Local Authority and Allied Personal Social Services,* Cmnd. 3703, HMSO July 1968; paragraphs 73 – 86.
6. Ibid, para. 91.
7. *The Government's Expenditure Plans* 1978/79 to 1981/82, Cmnd. 7049, HMSO January 1978; table 12.
8. Cmnd. 3703, para. 146.
9. Cmnd. 6233, para.
10. Ibid, para. 2.22.
11. Ibid, para. 4.18.
12. Ibid, para. 11.8.
13. Ibid, para. 11.5.
14. Ibid, para. 11.7.
15. *Priorities for the Health and Personal Social Services,* HMSO 1976, para. 8.11.
16. DHSS LASSL (77)24.
17. *DHSS Planning Guidelines* 1978/79, LAC(78)6, table 4.2.
18. Cmnd. 6233, para. 11.8.
19. Priorities Document. Page 83.
20. Ibid, para. 7.10.

PART EIGHT

THE ROLE OF THE VOLUNTARY SECTOR

11: Role of the Voluntary Sector in the Provision of Accommodation and other Facilities for Mentally Ill and Mentally Handicapped People

John Barter

1. Changing Role

The need for a variety of facilities and services to enable patients in mental illness and mental handicap hospitals to return to the world outside was recognised by a number of voluntary societies in the two decades following the end of the Second World War. Recognition was influenced by the study of Dr. Russell Barton[1] into the characteristics of long-stay patients and his finding that the institutions in which they lived actually incapacitated them. Barton noted the "apathy, lack of initiative, loss of interest more marked in things and events not immediately personal or present, submissiveness, and sometimes no expression of feelings of resentment at harsh or unfair orders". "There is also a lack of interest in the future and an apparent inability to make practical plans for it, a deterioration in personal habits, toilet and standards generally, a loss of individuality, and a resigned acceptance that things will go on as they are – unchanging, inevitably, and indefinitely".

In the early 1950s when Barton wrote his penetrating analysis of the paralysing effect of long stays in mental hospitals, there was no great concern to rehabilitate patients, and long-stay wards were thought to be eminently suitable resting places for many patients.

It is clear that Barton's work together with the changing concepts of the task of mental hospitals greatly influenced some members of the mental health professions and a number of thoughtful lay people. Not being prepared to wait until the statutory authorities made proper provision for rehabilitation of mental patients, they began to join voluntary societies which existed to promote the cause of mental health. Pre-eminent among these was the National Association for Mental Health (NAMH) formed in 1946.

In different parts of the country, frequently inspired by psychiatrists, nurses and social workers, local associations for mental health (LAMH) were formed for the purpose of providing services to enable mental patients to leave hospital and to live reasonably satisfying lives outside. The growth of LAMHs was fairly slow until the 1960s and 1970s when a rapid expansion took place, perhaps as a reaction to the failure of the great reforming Mental Health Act of 1959 (MHA '59) to inspire local authorities to set up comprehensive rehabilitation and after-care services. Most of these LAMHs went into business to set up group homes or clubs for former patients of mental illness hospitals. The voluntary sector has been much slower to provide after-care services for mentally handicapped people, giving greater priority to supporting and representing families with mentally handicapped members.

Alternative Services for Mentally Handicapped People

It is no accident that the foremost voluntary body concerned exclusively with mental handicap, the National Society for Mentally Handicapped Children (NSMHC) is a "relative group". NSMHC has set up three training establishments and four residential homes.

Many professionals who work in mental handicap hospitals seem to have been far less convinced than their colleagues from mental illness hospitals, by the arguments in favour of reducing the populations of such hospitals and returning patients to live with families or in smaller units outside hospital.[2] This probably reflects the feeling that severely mentally handicapped people, further incapacitated by long stays in hospital, require intensive care and support to survive outside. It is widely believed that only statutory bodies can afford the more expensive to build and run hostels, training establishments and day centres which severely mentally handicapped people are thought to need.

As the voluntary bodies and charities active in the mental health field are generally impoverished, compared to larger charities concerned with children or elderly people, wide-scale provision of capital and staff-intensive facilities is beyond their scope.

Although one or two pioneering LAMHs have run group homes for mentally handicapped people for some time, others are only beginning to experiment with group homes for such persons. It is vital, in understanding the part played by voluntary bodies in providing accommodation for former patients, to be aware of the key influence of mental health professionals, particularly psychiatrists. Because the professionals have not been convinced of the viability of group homes and other low-cost provision for mentally handicapped people, the voluntary section has hesitated for a very long time before implementing the radical notion of self-care by severely mentally handicapped people.

Services for Mentally Ill People

Contrast this conservative approach with the increasing radicalism of the voluntary movement in respect of mentally ill people. With professional encouragement and backing, group home projects have proliferated. At present there are over 400 in existence, providing over 1,700 places. Clubs, day centres, play groups, day nurseries and befriending schemes for mentally ill people and their families have also been established. From providing to campaigning is a fairly short step, so it is not surprising to find that the NAMH (now called 'MIND' following its first major campaign under that title, brilliantly run by David Ennals – destined to become Secretary of State for Social Services) is a major pressure group on behalf of mentally ill and mentally handicapped people and their families. MIND's campaigns are largely directed towards the closure of large, remote mental hospitals and the development of community psychiatric services and a full range of rehabilitative and after-care facilities in every local authority area. It has to be recognised that voluntary groups cannot conceivably supply such a comprehensive service, although they can and do contribute massively to certain parts of it. However, only a concerted effort over many years by the NHS and local authorities, augmented and inspired by the voluntary movement, can make comprehensive community care and effective rehabilitation a reality. In the meantime, voluntary bodies are making supreme efforts to show what can be done.

2. Diversity of Approach

The most important characteristic of the voluntary sector is its diversity, this has allowed a number of alternative methods of provision to emerge, provided mentally ill people with choice, and gives the statutory sector an opportunity of assessing the most appropriate mix of different types of accommodation and other services.

To illustrate this diversity there follows a description of the work of three widely differing voluntary bodies:

(a) The Mental After Care Association

The Mental After Care Association provides approximately 420 beds for the care of mentally ill people. It has eight long-stay homes along the south coast, catering for residents aged between 35 and 75 who remain for as long as is necessary, some for the remainder of their lives. It also has five after-care hostels, three of them in London. The aim of the hostels is to re-establish former mental patients in the community or, at least, to enable them to find employment and to play a full part in the world outside. The fourth hostel at Ipswich, aims to help young chronically ill people and those suffering from personality disorders requiring a large degree of guidance and support. This hostel incorporates a small workshop and indicates a growing consciousness within the voluntary movement of the crucial importance of training and employment in the resettlement of chronically mentally ill people.

(b) Psychiatric Rehabilitation Association

The Psychiatric Rehabilitation Association has set up the Community Housing Association, which runs six group homes in North and East London. Three of these were established and are managed in conjunction with senior community nursing staff from Claybury Hospital. The experience gained shows that given the right environment, chronic mentally ill patients continue to improve after leaving hospital, given a fuller life in the community. This has necessitated, not only the provision of accommodation, but in addition, such supportive setting as Industrial Units, Evening Groups, Holiday Schemes, a Restaurant Club etc. PRA's more recent experience has shown that the existence of a nearby Restaurant Club has enabled the less domestic patient to be discharged from hospital to be assured of proper nourishment and social work support by attending the restaurant, whilst relearning the art of domesticity.

(c) Cyrenians

It is not only the specialist mental health charities which are meeting the need of mentally ill people for accommodation. The National Cyrenians, whose purpose is to service the affiliated groups (27) which provide accommodation and support for homeless, single people. Collectively the local groups have 37 houses, 10 night shelters and 4 day centres around the country. It is probable that at least 30% of their residents have suffered from mental illness, and many are still in need of psychiatric help.

Unlike many hostels, few Cyrenian houses set limits on the length of time residents may remain. The Cyrenian ideal is to share responsibility between residents and workers, to evolve a group capable of making its own decisions and of providing a warm, sharing environment. In choosing new residents, selection rests on the individual's needs for a house, his likely compatability with existing residents and his ability to contribute to the group.

The skills of residents to manage their own affairs are developed in several ways, firstly through the weekly 'House Meeting' which aims to deal with the business of the house; secondly by offering a safe milieu for the discussion of personal and interpersonal matters; and thirdly by fostering group participation.

Besides providing services for single homeless people, Cyrenians are a campaigning body who were partly responsible for recent improved legislation on homelessness. However, the Housing (Homeless Persons) Act 1977, does not provide homeless single people with all the rights and protection Cyrenians deem appropriate.

3. The Voluntary Sector in Perspective

During 1976, MIND, assisted by the weekly journal "Community Care", carried out a postal survey of mental illness hospitals with the idea of obtaining factual material on their rehabilitation programmes and resources for long-stay patients, defined as people who had spent one year or longer in hospital.[3] Returns were obtained from 84 hospitals in England and Wales, providing 64% of the total population in mental illness hospitals.

The hospitals were asked to give an indication of the number of long-stay patients discharged to each of six types of accommodation in the previous year. These were:—

— own family

— local authority accommodation for mentally ill people

— voluntary run accommodation for mentally ill people

— general hostels

— old people's homes

— ordinary housing

It is significant that 29 hospitals had no record of where their long-term patients went, and many others were able to make only an estimate. Given the inadequacy of the data, only general impressions can be obtained from this survey. About 250 patients were discharged to accommodation run by voluntary bodies, considerably fewer than the numbers returning to their own families or discharged to old people's homes, but about twice as many as were discharged to either ordinary housing or to local authority accommodation for mentally ill people.

This survey tends to confirm the impression that without the aid given by families of mentally ill people and by the voluntary movement, the already inadequate statutory rehabilitation services would be quite unable to cope.

The survey revealed a most interesting development. It showed that several hospitals have established their own rehabilitation and accommodation services, notably the Littlemore Hospital (Oxford)[4], and the joint Herrison Hospital/Dorset County Council/District Housing Committee[5], much praised by the Hospital Advisory Service. A number of hospitals and social services departments are emulating the lead given by the Guideposts Trust and MIND, and are developing their own group home schemes. Once again, the innovatory work of voluntary societies is being picked up and developed by statutory authorities, which is an eminently proper relationship between the two sectors.

4. The Size of the Voluntary Sector's Contribution

(a) Homes and Hostels for Mentally Ill People*

The Government White Paper "Better Services for the Mentally Ill" (1975) provided tentative guidelines on provision of places in homes and hostels. In England and Wales some 11,000 places were thought to be needed. In 1975, 24 out of the 106 local authorities in England and Wales provided no accommodation for mentally ill people. The total number of places provided directly by local authorities in that year was 2,826 in 280 premises. In the same year the voluntary sector provided 894 places in 41 premises, excluding the small unstaffed premises known as group homes. MIND's local associations for mental health have 160 group homes, providing about 800 places. The total provision of accommodation by the voluntary sector for mentally ill people in 1975 was around 2,000 places, forming 41% of the total number of places available. In addition, the private sector in 1975 offered 472 places in 26 premises.

(b) Homes and Hostels for Mentally Handicapped People*

In 1975 local authorities in England and Wales provided 7,783 places in 403 premises, while the private and voluntary sectors together had 4,473 places,

---

* 'Mental Health Statistics for 1975' – MIND (1977) – largely derived from the Government's own statistics.

making a total of 10,946. This fell a long way short of the total of 34,300 places required by mentally handicapped children and adults, as estimated by the authors of the White Paper "Better Services for the Mentally Handicapped".

(c) Day Centres for Mentally Ill People*

The DHSS guidelines suggested that 64 day centre places were required per 100,000 population. In 1975 local authorities in England and Wales provided 3,673 places in 108 premises, a long way short of the 28,000 places thought to be needed. There are very many day centres and clubs run by voluntary societies but national statistics on the voluntary sector's contribution are not available. MIND's local associations have over 20 day centres and 110 social clubs for people recovering from mental illness, providing well over 1,000 places.

The Psychiatric Rehabilitation Association was among the first of the voluntary organisations to provide day centre facilities for chronic schizophrenic patients, and, based on a 5 day week. The emphasis of their approach to day centres has been education and re-education, rather than diversion. However, day centres and clubs run by voluntary bodies are seldom open five days each week or longer, whereas most statutory day centres give a five day service each week.

5. Evaluating the Voluntary Sector's Contribution

There is a dearth of published research on the efficacy and outcomes of residential provision made by voluntary agencies. This makes it difficult to combat the assertion increasingly being heard that hostels and homes can be as institutional as any hospital ward.

There are very real difficulties in reducing the ill-effects of corporate living noted by Dr. Barton. For example, the interim research report[6] on a hostel run by MIND for seriously disturbed young people, indicates that the stated aim of establishing in the community young people who have spent most of their lives in hospital, residential schools, children's homes or penal institutions, is not being entirely achieved. Only a third of the young people concerned are being rehabilitated, the remainder return to another institution, or they merely drift away. This is sobering data that should give pause to those who claim, as an article of faith, that voluntary provision is "better" than that of statutory bodies.

* 'Mental Health Statistics for 1975' – MIND (1977) – largely derived from the Government's own statistics.

Martin Weinberg, resident director of Pengwern Hall, an experimental training unit specialising in provision for mentally handicapped adolescents claims to have developed a "module of a system of life-time care for 80 people" which avoids the worst aspects of both institutionalisation and what he calls "the ghetto existence" of mentally handicapped people in the community.[2]

Lufton Manor[7], an NSMHC rural training unit in Somerset, has placed more than 50% of its people in open employment, a very much better result than those achieved by local authority training units. If getting and holding onto a job is an indication of success, and I believe it is, Lufton Manor has managed to avert some of the disabilities unwittingly inflicted upon residents by hospitals.

Using the same criterion, PRA's Plastics (and Developments) Limited, a Company with charitable status running Industrial Education Centres, has successfully employed mentally ill people in its own units, placed others in sheltered employment in factories, and has enabled others to move on to full time work, including some in the field of plastics.

The success of this project has lead to the formation of PRA Aids for the Handicapped Limited, which is enabling psychiatric patients to be of social service.[8] PRA has also used success in employment to measure the work of the Community Housing Association group homes[9], but in more recent years and particularly in conjunction with a joint project between PRA and the Cheshire Foundation, it has shown the value of accommodation and other supports as a possible alternative to hospital care, and to lessen the effect on the personality of institutionalisation. PRA has also developed the hostel as a "launching pad" into group homes and, in the event of relapse that may not require hospital admission, or where a hospital is reluctant to make a bed available, the group home resident is able to return to the hostel to enable more supportive care until recovery.

An unpublished survey carried out by the Information Officer of the Cyrenians tended to show that hostels for women in Leeds were reluctant to take, or to persevere with, very disturbed women or those with profound behavioural problems.[10]

A recent study for the Volunteer Centre of the work of two local associations for mental health[11] concluded that group homes were extensions of hospital rehabilitation practices. This was seen as helpful to patients making the transition from mental hospitals to the world outside. The author seemed to be saying that group homes seldom operate as a family; some of the authority under which the groups worked lay outside the home in hospital staff or the social services or the volunteers who supported the group in the house.

Peter Ryan and John Wing elsewhere in this book report their findings of a comparative study of group homes run by voluntary bodies and staffed hostels for mentally ill people run by local authorities in London. Their findings, that about 70% of the residents of staffed hostels could have been adequately accommodated in vastly less expensive group homes, may indicate that machinery is needed to ensure that mentally ill people are actually housed in the type of dwelling best suited to their needs.

More comparative research is urgently needed. Equally important we require careful assessments of the attitudes of staff caring for mentally ill or mentally handicapped residents in staffed homes and hostels, such as is being undertaken as part of the Pembroke Experiment. There is a great need for investigation into the way decisions are made in residential homes and hostels, to determine whether staff are any better than their colleagues in mental illness and mental handicap hostels at creating opportunities for residents to make real choices concerning their clothing, diet, activities within the establishment, their relationships, their living and sleeping conditions, and the maintenance of the fabric of the building.

6. The Housing Corporation and Voluntary Societies

The most exciting recent development in providing accommodation of various sorts for mentally ill and mentally handicapped people has been the interest shown by the Housing Corporation in encouraging housing and hostel schemes for people with special needs. In a circular[12] to all registered housing associations issued in December 1977, the Housing Corporation reiterated its policy that people with special needs should be fitted into ordinary self-contained housing wherever possible. The Corporation went on to say that financial help would henceforth be available to housing associations wishing to set up "supportive hostels", subject to certain limitations and safeguards. The registered housing association must be able to demonstrate that the additional "caring" costs above the normal hostel allowances will be met either by other statutory authorities or from charitable sources, and reasonable assurances of continuity will be required – normally a minimum of three years funding, including one year's notice of withdrawal.

The circular went on to advise housing associations to work on a two-tier basis with voluntary agencies who specialise in helping and rehabilitating people with social, mental or physical disadvantages. To ensure that schemes funded by either the Corporation or local authorities are an integral part of local provision, they should normally be agreed with the local housing authority and the social services department.

The Housing Corporation[13] is a semi-autonomous body set up in 1964, with extended powers under the 1974 Housing Act. Since this Act came into force, the main source of housing association finance has been the Housing Association Grant (HAG) which is paid by the Department of the Environment to enable housing associations to undertake new schemes, and a system of "deficit grants", also paid by the Department of the Environment, to cover any unavoidable shortfall between the housing association's income and its essential expenditure.

HAG is a once-and-for-all capital grant, covering 75% or more of either building a new hostel or restoring and repairing an existing building. The housing association charges its tenants a rent which they either pay from their own income, or may be paid from Supplementary Benefit, by social services departments, or by various combinations from these sources. To ensure the rent is a fair one, the rent officer is generally called in. It is important to note that the Housing Corporation is totally committed to the idea of fully integrating mentally ill and mentally handicapped people into normal housing, and to the avoidance of enclaves of people with special need. Nevertheless, some mentally ill or mentally handicapped people may best be served by being together in a small group in an unobtrusive house, where their shared skills will enable the group to survive and develop. Others will require the degree of support and help offered by a warden supervising a small group of dwellings; and for some, a warden or social worker living in the house or hostel may be the only viable alternative to remaining in hospital or going into a highly expensive and intensively staffed local authority home or hostel.

An interesting example of the way in which the Housing Corporation, a housing association and a voluntary body collaborated to provide "special needs" accommodation for mentally ill people comes from the London Borough of Brent. The Brent People's Housing Association, supported by the Brent Association for Mental Health, converted a large house into seven one or two-person self-contained flats. Tenants are people discharged from a large psychiatric hospital situated outside the borough. The former patients are supported by local volunteers with the social services departments and local psychiatric services providing necessary back-up. At least eight other schemes of this nature were in the offing early in 1977.

More importantly still, at least one Housing Association has made provision for mentally handicapped people. The Community Housing Association in Camden have a nine-bedroom converted Victorian terrace house with a big kitchen and sitting room. Initially, seven mentally handicapped people moved in, with two non-handicapped people who were carefully chosen and who are able to give some social support. The local Society for Mentally Handicapped Children is giving essential back-up support.

Guidance on housing mentally handicapped people is given in "Mentally handicapped people living in ordinary houses and flats", published by the Centre on Environment for the Handicapped.[14]

7. Political Action

For many years the more traditional voluntary bodies set great store by the provision of facilities for mentally ill and mentally handicapped people. They were, and still are, filling serious gaps in statutory provision. In many cases, voluntary societies experimented with new ways of meeting need, such as the Brent and Camden housing schemes described above. Because mentally ill and mentally handicapped people have not constituted a high political priority either in Parliament or in most local authorities, they have had to make do with second-rate and archaic services. Large, old-fashioned and remote mental hospitals continue to meet the bulk of the accommodation needs of these two groups of people. Consequently, charities such as NSMHC, MIND, PRA, and more recently, the National Schizophrenia Fellowship (NSF) have developed functions usually associated with pressure groups, so far without attracting the displeasure of the Charity Commissioners!

Mental illness is ubiquitous (one in ten people are likely to require hospital treatment for mental illness during their lives), while severe mental handicap continues to affect many thousands of people, despite the availability of new screening devices, immunisation techniques and knowledge about environmental causes.[15] Statutory provision, even though well supplemented by the voluntary sector, is completely inadequate at present. Quite unacceptable variations in provision between local authorities remain.

It is small wonder that the voluntary societies are putting political pressure on Parliamentarians and members of local authorities to give community services for mentally ill and mentally handicapped people the highest possible priority and to make those priorities stick! Heavy emphasis is placed on the need to provide a full range of accommodation and of day care, retraining and education facilities.

Striking examples of this campaigning approach are provided by the MIND campaign of the early 1970s and the 1977 MIND "Home From Hospital Campaign", which was supported by the Government to the tune of £20,000. It is estimated that this campaign, wonderfully supported by the media, particularly Granada TV, yielded 123 definite placements in lodgings or foster homes, and 300 additional group home places. How many other people offered lodgings or foster homes to local authorities direct as a result of the campaign is not known. It is clear that the campaign was also a major element in the development of "special needs" projects by housing associations.

The major voluntary bodies are represented on the mental health planning groups of at least two of the major political parties, where they press the case for more, and improved, day care and accommodation for mentally ill people. Despite financial pressures, local authorities are, by and large, giving financial help to local voluntary groups which provide accommodation, clubs, sheltered workshops and day centres. Such grants are, however, usually ludicrously small in relation to both the services given and the unmet need in most areas. There are some glowing examples of good practice, however, among them the social service department of Newcastle, the London Boroughs of Camden, Croydon and Hackney, and Dorset County Council.

But it is the Central Government that has at last recognised the importance of a strong voluntary movement in the field of mental health. With increasing complexity and the technical know-how that good local schemes now entail, the need for strong, well-informed and well-resourced national voluntary bodies to assist, advise, and finance local groups, as well as to give them a powerful national voice, cannot be over-estimated. Because mental health, as a general concept, has small fundraising appeal, major national charities have to rely heavily upon the DHSS for the funds to maintain a national presence and the provision of back-up for local groups. Financial exigencies and practical necessity have led to a fascinating, if often rather tense collaboration between the DHSS, national voluntary bodies, local voluntary groups, AHAs and local authorities.

It has been made clear that devices such as the relatively new joint-financing scheme, urban aid, housing action grants and central Government research monies are to be made available to voluntary bodies. Schemes or research employing all these various funding mechanisms are already in existence and can be expected to grow in number. Unfortunately, joint planning involving voluntary societies as a right is still a comparative rarity. Statutory authorities continue to be frightened of lay and consumer involvement in detailed planning of services, again with some honourable exceptions. Outworn prejudices about the 'amateurism' or 'unreliability' of volunteers and voluntary bodies unaccountably persist in local authorities and in AHAs.

The voluntary sector makes a contribution at least as large as social services, measured in man-hours[16] and, as has been shown here, makes a very substantial contribution to care and rehabilitation of mentally ill and mentally handicapped people. It is plain that the bastions of prejudice must fall, allowing the voluntary movement to take its rightful place as a full and contributing member alongside central Government, the consumers, local government and AHAs, in planning and providing services outside hospitals.

Notes and References

1. Barton, R. (1966), *Institutional Neurosis,* John Wright & Sons Ltd., 2nd edition.
2. For example: Martin Weinberg, 'Pengwern Hall – life time care for the mentally handicapped', *Social Work Today,* Vol. 8, No. 44, 10.8.77.
3. Murray, Joanna (1977), 'Better Prospects – A Report on Facilities in 84 Hospitals', MIND, 22 Harley Street, London, W1N 2ED.
4. Leopoldt, H., 'Sheltered accommodation for the mentally ill', *Nursing Mirror,* 22.1.76.
5. 'Room to Let: a report on 9 lodgings schemes', MIND Report No. 15, September 1978.
6. Unpublished research report by the Tavistock Institute of Human Relations (1978).
7. Carter, David, 'Not all Rural Training is Exploitation', *Residential Social Work,* Vol. 16, No. 7, July 1976.
8. Self Help in Psychiatry – PRA, London.
9. Croney, J. and Morgan, M., Group Homes for Mental Patients, PRA, London.
10. For further information contact Gordon Mathews, Cyrenians, Canterbury.
11. Dartington, T., 'Volunteers and Psychiatric Aftercare', Volunteer Centra, June 1978.
12. 'Joint Funding Arrangements for Caring Hostel Projects', Circular 1/77 (December 1977) – *Housing Corporation,* 149 Tottenham Court Road, London W1P 0BN.
13. 'Special Projects: Through Housing Associations', *National Federation of Housing Associations,* 86 Strand, London, WC2R 0EG.
14. Centre on Environment for the Handicapped, 126 Albert Street, London, NW1 7NF.
15. Clark, A. D. B. and Clark, Ann (1976), New Approaches in Mental Subnormality, MIND.
16. *Report of the Wolfendon Committee,* 'The Future of Voluntary Organisations', London, 1978.

APPENDIX — Addresses of some of the Voluntary Organisations concerned with Mentally Ill or Mentally Handicapped People

1. **Campaign for the Mentally Handicapped**
   96 Portland Place, London, W1N 4EX. Tel: 01-636 5020.

2. **CHAR**
   The Basement, 15 Cleveland Square, London, W.2. Tel: 01-723 2749.

3. **The Cyrenians Ltd.**
   13 Wincheap, Canterbury, Kent, CT1 3TB. Tel: Canterbury 51641.

4. **The Guideposts Trust Ltd.**
   74 High Street, Witney, Oxon. Tel: Witney 72885.

5. **The Mental After Care Association**
   Eagle House, 110 Jermyn Street, London, SW1Y 6H8.
   Tel: 01-839 5953.

6. **MIND**
   22 Harley Street, London, W1N 2ED. Tel: 01-637 0741.

7. **National Schizophrenia Fellowship**
   79 Victoria Road, Surbiton, Surrey, KT6 4NS. Tel: 390 3651/2/3.

8. **National Society for Mentally Handicapped Children**
   Pembridge Hall, 17 Pembridge Square, London, W2 4EP.
   Tel: 01-229 8941.

9. **Psychiatric Rehabilitation Assoc.**
   The Groupwork Centre, 21a Kingsland High Street, Dalston,
   London, E.8. Tel: 01-254 9753.

10. **Richmond Fellowship**
    8 Addison Road, London, W14 8DL. Tel: 01-603 6373/4/5.

11. **The Spastics Society**
    12 Park Crescent, London, W1N 4EQ. Tel: 01-636 5020.

Contributors

John Barter	Deputy Director, MIND.
Dr. Christine Hassall	Senior Research Fellow, Department of Psychiatry, University of Birmingham.
Dr. Sheila Hewett	Currently Social Worker, Nottingham County Council Social Services Department, previously Member of the Scientific Staff, M.R.C. Social Psychiatry Unit.
Alan Holden	Principal Officer, Forward Planning Section, Development Division, Coventry Social Services Department.
M. Rolf Olsen	Director of Social Work Courses, Professor of Social Work, University of Birmingham.
Peter Ryan	Research Social Worker, M.R.C. Social Psychiatry Unit, Institute of Psychiatry.
Helen Slater	Former Social Worker, Exe Vale Hospital, and former Secretary, Exeter Council for Social Service.
Gertrude Smith	Retired. Former Part-time Lecturer, Portsmouth Polytechnic and Psychiatric Social Worker, The Old Manor Hospital, Salisbury.
Tom White	Director of Social Services, City of Coventry.
John K. Wing	Director, M.R.C. Social Psychiatry Unit, Institute of Psychiatry.